TO ELIZABETH DUBACH   6-19-96

FROM John F Bassen

6-19-96

THE ARTIST WAS A YOUNG MAN

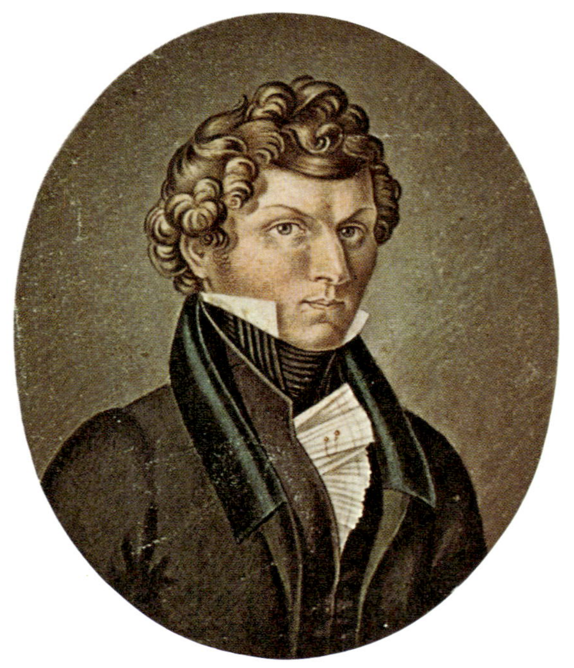

Self-portrait of the artist at age 28 [Untitled].
This miniature has remained in the family since the artist's demise.
Watercolor, 3½ x 2⅞ inches (actual size), 1833/1834.
Courtesy of Mrs. Frances Rindesbacher Eustice, Cleveland Heights, Ohio.

THE ARTIST WAS A YOUNG MAN

The Life Story of Peter Rindisbacher
by **ALVIN M. JOSEPHY, JR.**

ACCOMPANYING EXHIBITION PRESENTED AT:
AMON CARTER MUSEUM, FORT WORTH
NATIONAL GALLERY OF CANADA, OTTAWA
CITY ART MUSEUM OF ST. LOUIS, ST. LOUIS
GLENBOW-ALBERTA INSTITUTE, CALGARY
ROYAL ONTARIO MUSEUM, TORONTO

AMON CARTER MUSEUM   **FORT WORTH**

The Amon Carter Museum was established in 1961 under the will of the late
Amon G. Carter for the study and documentation of westering North America.
The program of the Museum, expressed in publications, exhibitions, and
permanent collections, reflects many aspects of American culture, both
historic and contemporary.

LIBRARY OF CONGRESS CATALOG CARD NO. 75-101097 COPYRIGHT © 1970 AMON CARTER MUSEUM OF WESTERN ART
ALL RIGHTS RESERVED   LITHOGRAPHED IN USA

ACKNOWLEDGMENTS

The title suggested by the author, Alvin M. Josephy, Jr., implies the transience of
Peter Rindisbacher both as man and artist. There have been moments in research for both the
book and the accompanying exhibition when we wished for more assertive facts, better
documentation, and a greater corpus of the man's work upon which to base judgments. The
measure of our success is modest, yet we feel that we have met the man and know
something more of his life and work. That we close our effort with many questions yet
unanswered leaves a tantalizing challenge for other art historians.

Our effort has truly been a joint endeavor. Elizabeth Dally Eames of New York City,
descendant of Frederic Rindesbacher, younger brother of Peter, has contributed most
generously by her knowledge and enthusiasm for the family history and by guiding us to
many sources of information. We are indebted to the Reverend and Mrs. Peter Dally of Vashon
Island, Washington, and to Mrs. Frances Rindesbacher Eustice of Cleveland Heights,
Ohio, for unique examples of the artist's work hitherto unpublished and unknown to students
of American art.

For loans to both the exhibit and for permission to publish pictures in *American Heritage*
magazine we wish to thank the following: Mr. Harold Cate, La Crosse, Wisconsin; Glenbow-
Alberta Institute, Calgary; Mrs. Louis Gust, Lockport, Illinois; Mr. Louis T. Hall, Jr., El Dorado,
Arkansas; Hudson's Bay Company, Winnipeg; M. Knoedler & Company, Inc., New York;
Missouri Historical Society, St. Louis, Missouri; Public Archives of Canada, Ottawa; Pea-
body Museum of Archaeology and Ethnology, Cambridge, Massachusetts; Royal Ontario
Museum, Toronto; The State Historical Society of Wisconsin, Madison, Wisconsin; and West
Point Museum, West Point, New York.

With the cooperation of Mr. Josephy and the editors of *American Heritage* the
museum has been able to coordinate the exhibition and publication with a special feature
on Peter Rindisbacher prepared by Mr. Josephy for the February, 1970, issue.

The exhibition and accompanying publications have been assembled by Peter H. Hassrick and
Mrs. Sue Jacobson of the Amon Carter Museum staff.

Mitchell A. Wilder

CONTENTS

PLATES

*COLOR

PLATES *continued*

*COLOR

THE ARTIST WAS A YOUNG MAN

I. BOYHOOD IN SWITZERLAND

Among the major artists of Indian and frontier life in the early American and Canadian West probably the least familiar is Peter Rindisbacher, who was born in Switzerland in 1806 and died suddenly in St. Louis in 1834 at the age of 28.[1] In the museums, art galleries and auction houses, and among modern-day students and aficionados of the Western scene, the names and paintings of Karl Bodmer, George Catlin, Paul Kane and Alfred Jacob Miller strike chords of immediate recognition and response. But Peter Rindisbacher, whose work on many scores must place him firmly among them as an equal, has for generations been little known to the general public.

Some of Rindisbacher's picturesque and dramatically accurate drawings of Indian life in central Canada and the U. S.'s Old Northwest, reproduced in books and periodicals in the original or as lithographs, are so familiar today as to have become — as in the case of his buffalo-hunting scenes — almost standard images of the American Indian of the past. But for more than a century the artist himself has been little more than a name, eluding almost all attempts by occasional biographers to find out more about him.

Rindisbacher's career accounts for a large part of this obscurity. Transplanted at 15 from Switzerland to the remote and struggling Red River Colony in the Indian country of present-day Manitoba, he lived during the remainder of his short life among pioneer societies that were preoccupied with extending and securing civilization in the Red River and upper Mississippi River valleys. Some of his friends and neighbors in the several places in which he resided recognized his talents as a miniature portraitist and a painter of the scenes around him, and not a few of them admired the meticulous realism with which he portrayed subjects that were familiar to them. From time to time various of his Indian and Canadian views found their way to England and the eastern United States and were reproduced as lithographs or engravings. Although not all of them were credited to him, he began to receive attention in the last years of his life from editors and the general public. But his sudden and premature death cut short this widening notice, and the interest even of most of those who had known him personally waned quickly. Few of them had recognized the stature or significance of his work, and the *Missouri Republican* of St. Louis, which on August 15, 1834, briefly noted his passing, gave no facts about his life and said little more than that he "had talents which gave every assurance of future celebrity." In a short time the relatively small number of his Indian and Canadian scenes that the public had gotten to know were eclipsed by the works of Catlin and other newer and better-publicized artists who traveled to the West, and Rindisbacher became so forgotten that even some of those persons for whom he had rendered exquisite family miniature portraits lost remembrance of the name of the man who had painted them.

In a way, Rindisbacher's talents, which the *Missouri Republican* had noted at his death, were extraordinary: many of his paintings and drawings of Indians and Canadian fur posts and frontier life were done amid extreme perils and hardships when he was between the ages of 15 and 20. Although Rindisbacher died while his abilities as an artist were still maturing, he was a close observer of life and an expert draftsman, and his paintings and drawings, as works of art, have a vitality, youthful enthusaism, and richness of detail that inevitably excite those who see them. To the historian and ethnographer, moreover, his work is an invaluable record of a time and place that no one else pictured. He was the first artist to portray the Canadian West and first to depict many aspects of plains Indian life. The care and accuracy he gave to the details of his paintings rank them, for the student, with the work of Bodmer, Catlin, and numerous other artists of Indian and frontier life whom Rindisbacher preceded in the northern plains and westernmost woodlands of the continent by a decade or more.

Like most of those artists who followed him, Rindisbacher was an eyewitness of almost everything he depicted. On the Red River of the North in the vicinity of present-day Winnipeg and along the upper Mississippi River in Minnesota, Wisconsin and Illinois, he knew Cree,

Chippewa, Assiniboine, Sioux, Winnebago, and Sauk and Fox Indians, as well as halfbloods and white fur traders, and in the 1820's he observed their ways of wilderness life at first hand. But unlike almost all the other artists of the early West, he had not traveled deliberately into the Indian country on limited visits to observe and paint native ways. From Switzerland, he had been plumped down as a permanent resident in a far outpost of white colonization, deep in the heart of North America, in the midst of fur traders and warring Indian tribes, and as an actor thereafter in one of the strangest dramas of settlement in the history of the West, he had had an uninterrupted opportunity to record, year after year, the seasonal round of activities and scenes of the land in which he lived. As a result, his full artistic legacy, much of which is still only slightly known, provides a varied and significant documentation of the people, events and customs that he witnessed, from one season to the next, and is singularly free of such aberrations as Catlin's erroneous depiction of northern plains Indians garbed in summer dress while engaged in a winter buffalo hunt, an event that Catlin did not see and could only imagine.[2]

Today, thanks to the dedicated research of a number of persons who since the early 1930's have pursued various strands of Rindisbacher's life, much is now known concerning him.[3] He was born in the upper Emmenthal (the Valley of the Emme River) in the Canton of Berne, Switzerland, on April 12, 1806. The family name, Rindisbacher, it appears, was derived from the district's ancient court of "Rindisbach" and, in variously spelled forms, was a familiar one among the German-speaking burghers and farmers of the region. Peter's grandfather and father, both of whom were also named Peter, were members of the Reformed Lutheran Church.

In 1779 the grandfather married Elsbet Neuenschwander of Eggiwil and moved to that town in the upper Emme Valley. There, the artist's father was born on November 1, 1780, and grew up in one of a group of houses known as the Luchsmatt, which the family owned, on the Rotenbach River which flowed into the Emme at Eggiwil. In 1800 the father married Barbara (or Barbe) Ann Wyss of Biglin, and between 1801 and 1815 the couple, still living in the Luchsmatt, had five daughters and two sons. Peter, the future artist, baptised in Eggiwil on April 27, 1806, was the third child and the second son in the family.[4]

Contemporary Swiss records suggest that the Rindisbachers were neither rich nor poor. The father, like his father before him, was a farmer, but after 1806 he changed his principal occupation to that of a veterinary surgeon. Young Peter seems to have revealed a compelling interest in pictures and in drawing from his earliest years. Family stories tell of him "looking attentively at the paintings which represented the heroic past of his ancestors whose deeds were held up to him and left their stamp on his youth." By the time he was six years old, he was demonstrating his own abilities with crayons and charcoal, first receiving punishment for drawing with them on walls and doors in his home, and then incurring the displeasure of his teachers by filling his school copybooks with pictures. His grandparents disapproved of his preoccupation with drawing and urged his father to apply the boy to field work so as to make a "decent" farmer of him. But his father seems to have sympathized with young Peter's real inclination and, giving him paper, pencils and watercolors, encouraged him with his art.

Under his mother's tutelage, the boy learned, at the same time, to play the zither. But his interests also included the romance of Swiss history and the glory of military heroes and battles, which the many current stories and pictures of events of the Napoleonic wars made graphic to him. He learned to play the drum, and, when he was ten, attached himself as a drummer boy to a company of grenadiers in Berne. He fell out as a volunteer at musters of the company, and its members adopted him as something of a mascot and let him drum signals for them during their exercises and maneuvers. He sketched scenes of the musters and drew portraits of the grenadiers that delighted them, and once, it is said, they interceded protectively for him when he had angered a dragoon officer whom he had sketched unflatteringly. The picture, showing the officer sitting awkwardly on his horse, had not pleased its subject.

Only a few drawings which Peter made during his earliest years are known to exist today. One of them, reflecting the youth's interest in Swiss history, shows a theatrically muscular and bearded William Tell leaping to a shelf of rock.[5] Another, a torn remnant of a larger sketch, portrays French soldiers of Napoleon's army in the midst of a battle scene. Dead soldiers, drawn only in outline, lie all about and the drawing seems to have been copied from an engraving. If so, it suggests one of the methods by which the young artist may have been teaching himself to draw. As he often did later in his career when he made copies of his own drawings, he may have rubbed his pencil over the entire rear surface of an engraving, then placed it face up on his drawing paper, and traced the lines of the engraving with the pressure of a stylus-like instrument so that the picture would be reproduced on the fresh sheet of paper. Then he would have gone over the traced lines with a pencil or pen and added his own details.

When he was 12, Peter was sent by his father on a vacation trip to the Bernese Alps with a Swiss painter named Jacob S. Weibel, who gave the boy the only serious art training he was ever to receive. Weibel was a member of a school of Bernese miniature painters who specialized in small, carefully detailed landscapes and idyllic rural scenes. Under his instruction Peter drew views of the high Alps along the Italian border. Weibel's lessons left a strong imprint on the young artist, and the influence of the school of Bernese miniaturists can be seen in much of his work from that time on.

Peter's father, meanwhile, had changed the Rindisbacher family's place of residence. Various contemporary sources refer to Peter Sr. as a restless man.[6] When his own mother — the artist's grandmother — died in 1816, he had sold the Luchsmatt in Eggiwil and had bought a large farmhouse and surrounding property in Neiderwichtrach. This house did not suit Peter Sr. for long, however, and in 1818 he gave it up, moving his family several times again, from one residence to another, and finally settling into a house in Munsingen which he rented from two blacksmith brothers, Johannes and Samuel Burki. But he was still restless. In 1820 a recruiting agent for Lord Thomas Douglas, the fifth Earl of Selkirk, appeared in the neighborhood, seeking colonists for Selkirk's colony on the Red River, south of Lake Winnipeg in the interior of North America. The elder Rindisbacher was ready for another change and, responding to the promise of being able to better himself in the New World, signed to take his family across the Atlantic Ocean.

Although Selkirk's agent pictured the Red River Colony as happy and prosperous, it was anything but that. Selkirk had founded it in 1811 after having purchased from the Hudson's Bay Company, of which he was a major stockholder, a grant of some 116,000 square miles extending southward from Lake Winnipeg into the present-day states of North Dakota and Minnesota. In exchange, Selkirk had paid the fur company a token of ten shillings and had promised to settle a thousand families on the grant within ten years.[7]

The project was designed to fulfill aims of both Selkirk and the big British fur company. For some years the fortunes of the company had been declining. Dividends had fallen steadily and since 1809 had not even been declared; the company's stock had dropped from £ 250 to £50. Numerous operational changes and economies had been ordered, and in the field in Canada it was hoped that the traders and their employees would learn to live off the country and become less dependent on costly supplies sent them from England. The Red River was in the wilderness, far west of Canada's most advanced settlements. But it was strategically situated near the routes that many of the fur brigades followed in going between the posts on Hudson Bay and the fur-gathering countries to the west and north; and an industrious agricultural colony settled on the fertile land along the river could provide a cheap supply of food for the Hudson's Bay Company's men in the interior of the continent. Selkirk, on the other hand, had long been concerned over the hardships of impoverished peasants in Ireland and Scotland, particularly in the Scottish Highlands, where numerous crofters had been evicted from their homes to provide larger sheep runs for the big landowners, and he hit on emigration as the answer to their plight and the Red River in British America as the place for them to go.

All might have been well save for two things. The 116,000 square miles granted to Selkirk by the Hudson's Bay Company (which governed the region by royal charter) were the home and hunting grounds of many bands of Indians and families of French-speaking halfbloods, known as Métis, who got on well with the fur traders, but would be wary of, and even hostile to, people who settled on the land and drove away the game. And to make matters more ominous, within the territory of the grant lay several strong posts of the North West Fur Company, the bitter and powerful Montreal-based rival of the Hudson's Bay Company. The Nor'westers' posts were essentially food-supplying centers for their own traders and canoemen who gathered furs farther north and west in the Canadian wilds. On the plains near Red River, Métis and friendly Indians hunted buffalo, bringing in the meat to the forts where it was pounded and formed into packs of nourishing pemmican for the North West Fur Company men. An agricultural settlement placed by their rivals in their midst, the North West Company partners could see, might prove to be a disruptive threat to their own affairs.

Soon after Selkirk's colony was launched, the threat materialized. In 1811 an advance party of laborers was sent from England to Hudson Bay, and in August, 1812, under Selkirk's agent, Miles Macdonell, they reached Red River to set up the colony. At once Macdonell began to act in a high-handed manner toward the Nor'Westers and Métis, and at a "seizin' of the land" ceremony proclaimed himself governor of "Assiniboia," the name he gave to the territory of the grant. More settlers arrived from Scotland later in the fall of 1812, and a third group in 1813.

The tempers of the already resentful Méis flared higher as they watched surveyors lay out farms for the newcomers on land they considered their own. The colonists proved to be poor farmers, and in 1814, when starvation faced them, Macdonell began to requisition, and then

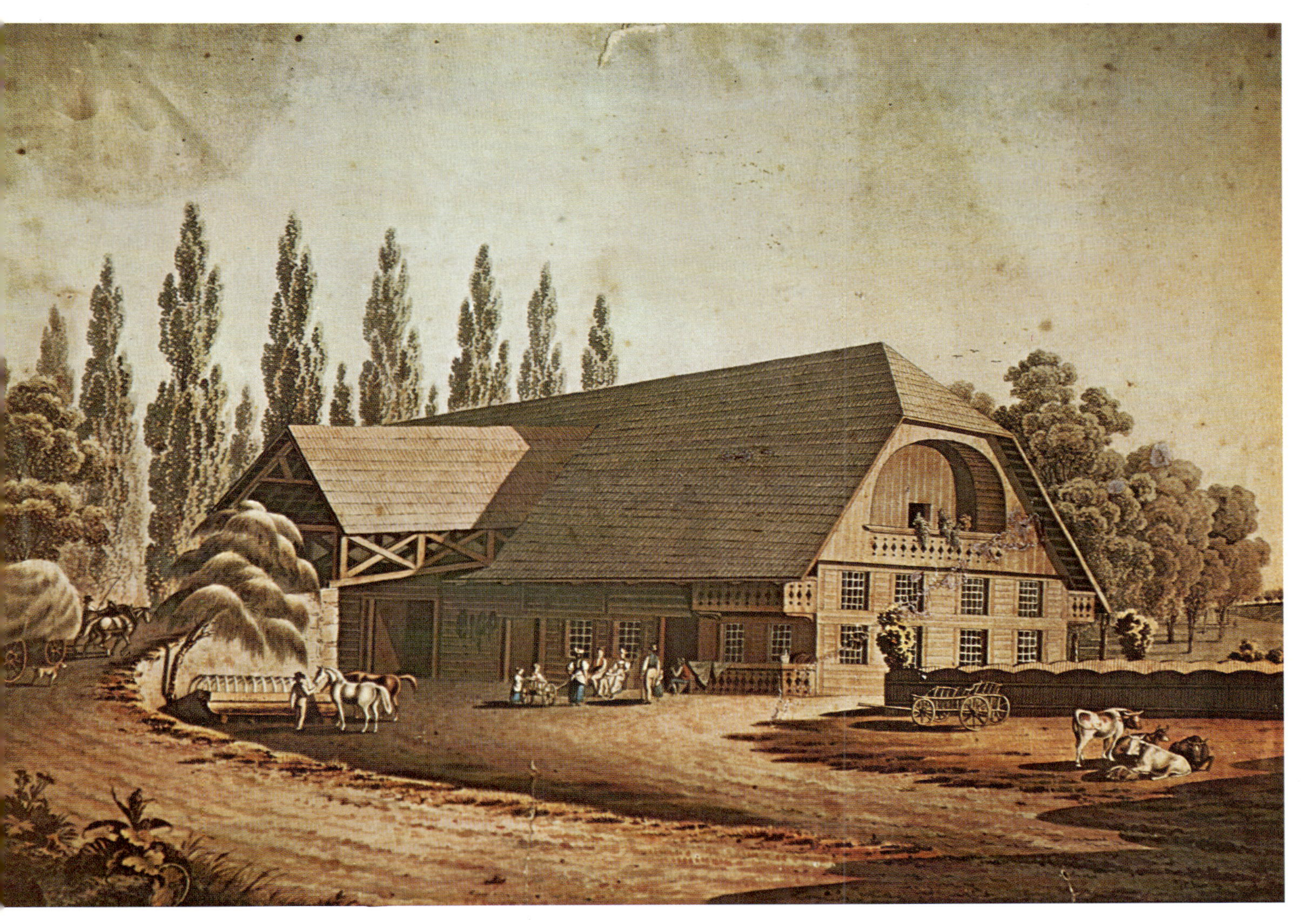

I. Old Swiss homestead of the Rindisbacher family in Munsinger [Untitled].
The painting was probably executed long after the Rindisbachers had moved
to the New World. Peter possibly did the watercolor from a sketch he
brought with him. The house stands today altered only slightly by time.
Watercolor, 8 x 11½ inches, ca. 1830.
Courtesy of Mrs. Mildred Rindesbacher Grimm, Rochelle, Illinois.

forcibly to seize, supplies of pemmican and other food belonging to the North West Company. Petty fighting soon erupted into a savage war between Macdonell, his colonists, and the Hudson's Bay Company on one side and the Métis and the North West Company on the other.

The conflict raged with increasing seriousness year after year. Men were ambushed in the wilds and killed; posts were captured, ransacked, and burned; in a battle fought on Red River twenty-three persons died, including the Hudson's Bay Company's governor-in-chief of Rupert's Land; and prominent leaders on both sides, including Lord Selkirk himself, were arrested and brought to trial. In the course of the struggle, the trade of both fur companies was thrown into turmoil, and Lord Selkirk's colony was brought several times to the brink of collapse. Twice, the Métis evicted the settlers, though each time they came back. In 1817 Selkirk recruited one hundred members of the disbanded de Meuron regiment, Swiss mercenaries who had fought for the British in Canada in the War of 1812, and took them from Montreal to the Red River as armed colonists to fight the Métis. Finally, by 1821, hostilities ended, and the two fur companies merged, the Hudson's Bay Company remaining dominant in the Red River area and taking over the former North West Company posts. Selkirk, who had almost become deranged during the bitter fighting, had died in Pau, France, on April 8, 1820, but the Red River Colony, shaken and far from stable, was still in existence.

Prior to his death, Selkirk had decided to recruit more colonists. Among the de Meuron veterans, he had met two Swiss officers from Berne, Lieutenant Friedrich von Graffenried von Burgistein and a Captain Rudolf von May,[8] and they seem to have influenced him to provide fellow-countrymen for the Swiss soldiers who had become permanent residents at the colony. At any rate, in 1819, Selkirk sent von May to Switzerland as a recruiting agent, and on January 8 of the following year von May petitioned officials in Berne for permission to enlist emigrants for the Selkirk colony on the Red River.

Although refusing to support the undertaking, the authorities put no obstacle in the way of any Swiss citizen who desired to emigrate, and von May set about the task of searching for likely prospects whom he could induce to leave their homeland for the distant colony. Pamphlets in both German and French, giving an enthusiastic but highly colored and exaggerated picture of the Red River area, its climate, soil, and prospects for newcomers, were produced and distributed, and in a series of meetings in the German-speaking Cantons of Neuchâtel, Vaud and Geneva deceptively rosy descriptions of the state of the settlement and the opportunities that lay there were given by von May to wrapt audiences of peasant families and townspeople.[9] By the spring of 1821, von May had recruited some fifty-seven adults and their families, promising each family head, or unmarried man over the age of 21, one hundred acres of land, seeds, cattle, and farming implements, for which they could pay with five hundred bushels of wheat after they had been in the colony for five years. Among the recruits in the Canton of Berne was the Rindisbacher family — father Peter, his wife, and six of their children, including the budding artist, young Peter. The oldest Rindisbacher child, Elizabeth, who would have been 20 at the time, may have been either married or dead; she did not accompany the family to America, and nothing is known of her.

Peter, who was now 15 years old, was already considered a talented draftsman. His self-portrait, which he drew at a later time in his life, shows that he had light-colored hair, blue eyes, a long nose and pronounced chin, and a serious, though not severe, expression. Comparisons of this portrait with those he did of his parents indicate that he resembled his mother more than his father. The latter, who was then 42 years old, was the senior member among all those who were emigrating, and he became known to them, in time, as Father Rindisbacher. Despite the surviving references to him, both in Switzerland and at the Red River Colony, as "restless" and "not steady," he was recalled by one of the colonists in later years as having possessed a "strong, forceful" character that made him the leader of the emigrants.[10]

On May 3, 1821, passports were issued at Berne for 165 persons,[11] and a week later the families assembled under von May's direction at Kaiser-Augst, a small village on the Rhine near Basel. Like the other families in the party, the Rindisbachers had disposed of, or left behind, all their possessions that were not deemed necessary for their new life. Some of their effects may eventually have been claimed by their Munsinger landlords, the Burki brothers, who, after the Rindisbacher's depature, announced that Peter Sr. had left Switzerland owing them 60 Kronen, the equivalent of about $210 dollars today.[12]

A few of the colonists wondered why von May had gathered them outside of Basel, rather than in the big, commercial city itself. Later, when disillusionment had set in as a result of the stern realities of life on Red River, the settlers persuaded themselves that the recruiting agent had "feared to take them to a large city, lest some unfavorable facts connected with the country to which they were going might come to light." [13] But amid the excitement of the departure, and with their minds filled with expectations of the fortunes they would make in the New

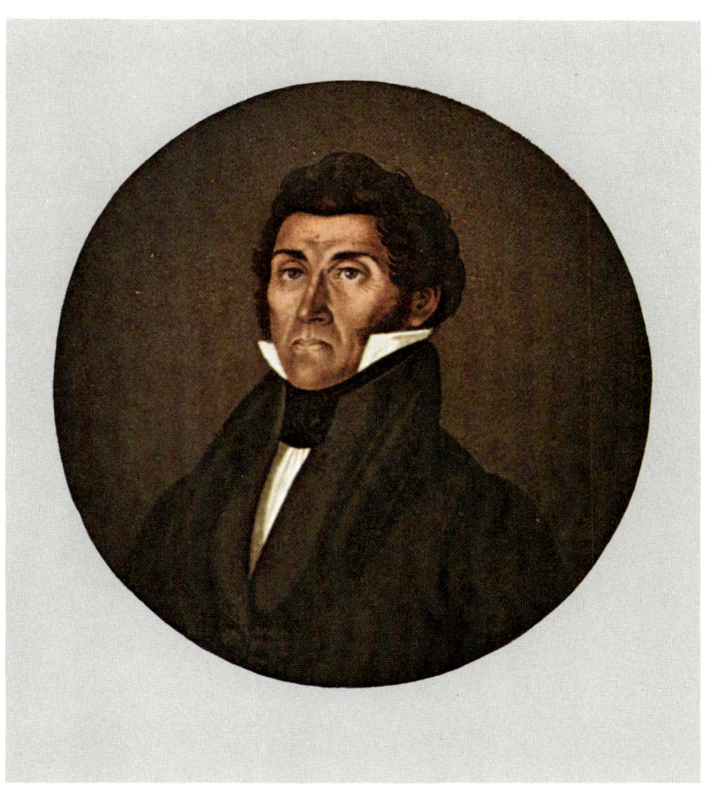

**II. Portrait of the artist's father,
Pierre Rindesbacher, Sr. (1779–1865) [Untitled].**
Watercolor, 3⁷⁄₁₆ x 3¼ inches (actual size), ca. 1825.
Courtesy of Mrs. Virginia Rindesbacher Feltmeyer, Stockton, Illinois.

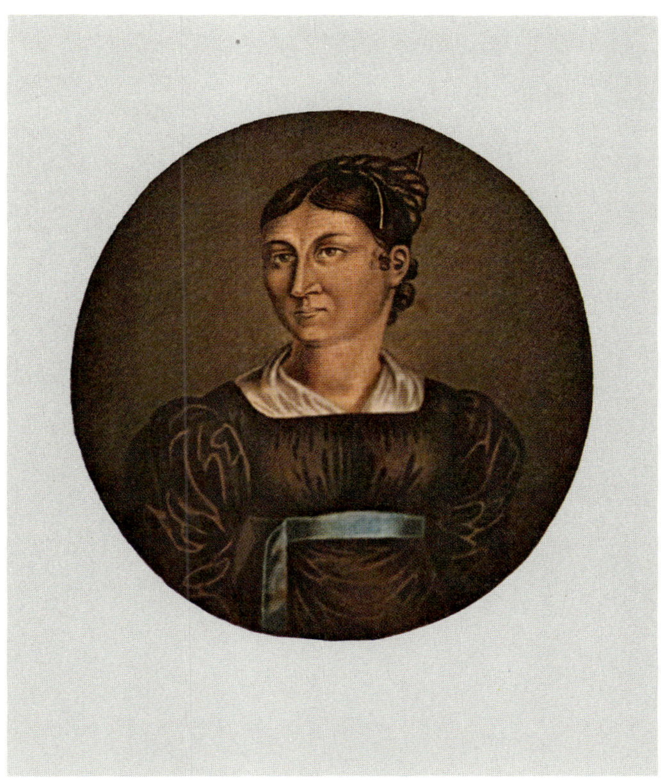

**III. Portrait of the artist's mother,
Barbara Ann [Barbe] Rindesbacher (ca. 1782–1832) [Untitled].**
Watercolor, 3 x 2⁷⁄₈ inches (actual size) ca. 1825.
Courtesy of Mrs. Virginia Rindesbacher Feltmeyer, Stockton, Illinois.

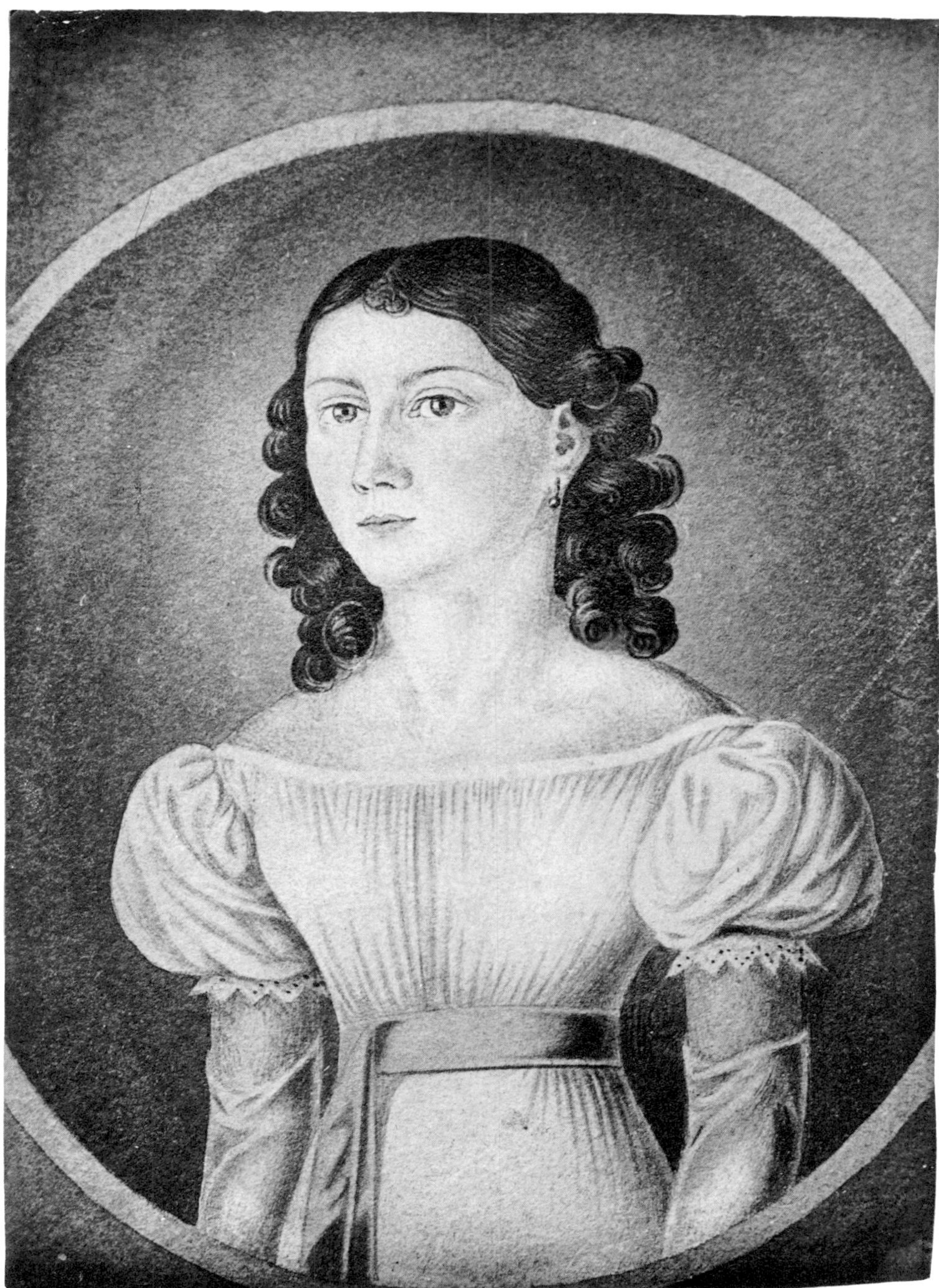

IV. Portrait of the artist's sister, Madaline Rindesbacher (1812–1859) [Untitled].
Photograph of an original watercolor painted ca. 1830, which has since been lost.
7⅞ x 5⁵⁄₁₆ inches.
Courtesy of Mrs. Louise A. Gust, Lockport, Illinois, and Mr. Harold H. Cate, LaCrosse, Wisconsin.

World, no one questioned the agent, and on May 10 the families set off with their baggage on two barges down the Rhine. Thirteen days later, they reached the Dutch port of Dordrecht, their embarkation point near Rotterdam, and were shown the ship that would take them to America, a three-masted English vessel, the *Lord Wellington*, of 415 tons.

II. TO CANADA

It is possible that while the Swiss families waited at Dordrecht, they were joined by other emigrants, for different contemporary sources give different figures, ranging from 165 to 187, of the number of colonists who actually sailed on the *Lord Wellington*. Somewhere, before their embarkation, the Rindisbachers themselves acquired another family member, a 2-year-old baby known today only as Gautier, whom they adopted and who is believed to have been of Welsh parentage. Whatever its total number actually was, the party as a whole included persons from Neuchâtel, Vaud, and Geneva, as well as Berne, Cantons. Three-fourths of the emigrants, in fact, were French-speaking Swiss, and some of them were descendants of Huguenot emigrés from eastern France.[14]

On May 30, just before their departure, Peter Sr., possibly acknowledged already as the leading member of the party, affixed his name first to a list of signers of a letter to friends and relatives in Switzerland that stated specifically that there were 180 emigrants in the group. The message, printed in the *Berner Wochenblatt (Berne Weekly)* on June 30, 1821, read:

> *Notice from the colony: 180 persons strong, which left for North America on May 10, 1821 from Kayser-Augst bey Basel, to relations, fellow countrymen and brothers.*
>
> On May 23 we arrived at the harbor of this place happy and safe and immediately settled near our English Transport, called 'Wellington' which was here. On the 24th we were directed to our places on that ship and we have enough space, and our vessel is provisioned for 10 months. Our supplies consist, until then, of bread, meat, bacon, brandy, butter, flour, peas, potatoes; more enough of all which will be little affected on shipboard; except, instead of bread, we have ship's bisquits. Since

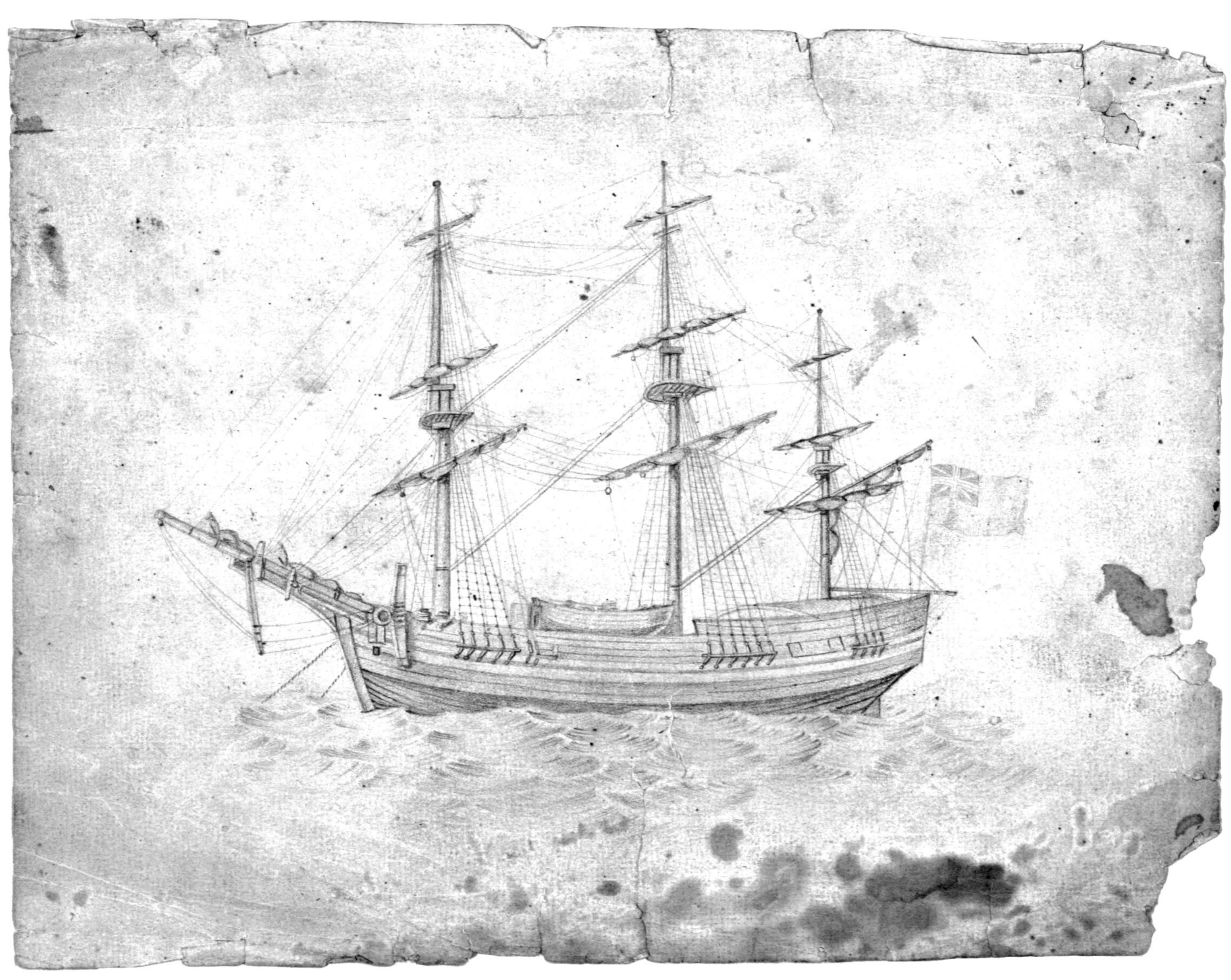

V. Side view of the *Wellington* [Untitled].
Pencil, 8⅞ x 11 inches, ca. 1821.
Courtesy of Mrs. Frances Rindesbacher Eustice, Cleveland Heights, Ohio.

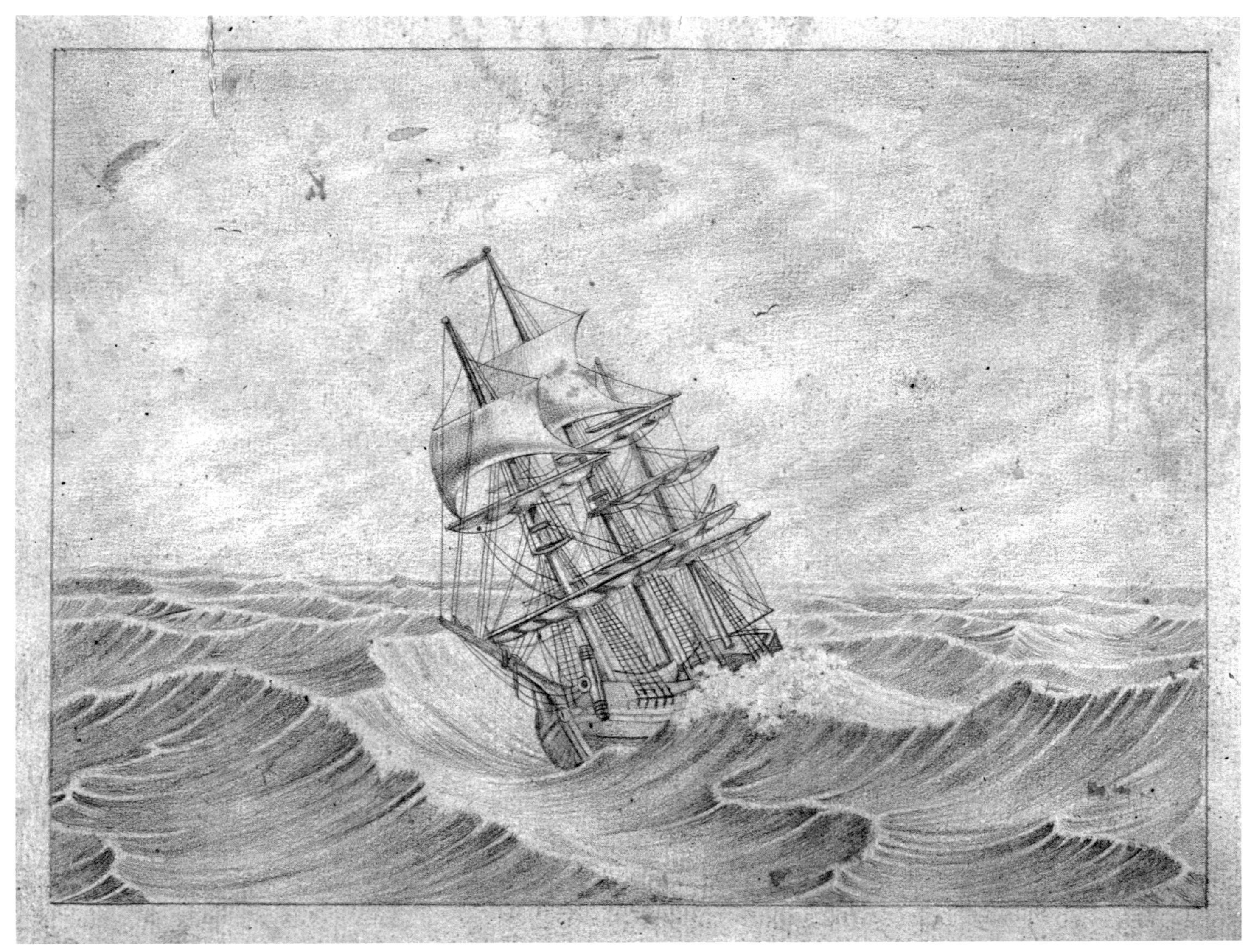

VI. Quarter view of the *Wellington* in high seas [Untitled].
Pencil, 8¹³⁄₁₆ x 11 inches, ca. 1821.
Courtesy of Mrs. Frances Rindesbacher Eustice, Cleveland Heights, Ohio.

our English provisioner [von May] is himself an inhabitant of the Red River, and has told us many good and lovely things about our new fatherland, so it seems that the achievement of our undertaking cannot be doubted.

Today at 2 o'clock we sail from here in best of health and with high spirits. Therefore we take leave of you, our countrymen and brothers, and wish you happiness and blessings; we especially express our satisfaction and thanks to the authorized commissioner of our colony, Captain von May. We hope that soon many of our compatriots will follow and enjoy, with us, the advantage of our new homeland.

In the Schiffszimmer [Captain's cabin] on the ship 'Wellington' in the harbor at Dortrecht on the 30th of May, 1821.

In the name of all the colonists:
Pierre Rindlisbacher [a variant spelling of the family name]
Christian Rothenbuhler
Christian Rychener
Aron Dubach
Johannes Dubach
Christian Aebersold
Ludwig Engel[15]

On the same day, the *Lord Wellington*, commanded by Captain James Falbister, set out to sea with its passengers. Like many emigrants to the New World before them, the Swiss colonists were an unlikely group to be heading for a pioneering life in the American wilderness. Most of them had been city-dwellers rather than farmers, and their skills were those of professional people and artisans—clockmasters, musicians, apothecaries, dentists, schoolmasters, and mechanics. But von May had carefully concealed from them the demanding nature of the frontier existence they faced, and their dreams were those of light-hearted travelers, rather than adventurers or pioneers.

The ship was bound for York Factory, the Hudson's Bay Company's big fur depot on the western shore of Hudson Bay, from where the colonists would proceed inland via an established fur trade route to Lake Winnipeg and Red River. Captain Falbister's course took the *Wellington* through the North Sea, past the Orkney Islands north of the British Isles, where the vessel paused briefly, and then south of Greenland to the entrance to Hudson Bay. In later years, Augustus L. Chetlain,[16] the son of Louis Chetlain, who was the head of one of the more prominent emigrant families, published an account of the colonists' adventures. Soon after they had left Dordrecht, he wrote, "it was found that the quality of the food issued was greatly inferior to that promised them before their departure from Switzerland, and complaint was made to the captain of the ship — a stern but kind-hearted old seaman, who acknowledged the wrong, but claimed that he was not responsible for it, which was no doubt true. The water also was bad, and issued in insufficient quantities."[17] It gave the colonists the first of their misgivings, but they were to have more of them, even before they reached Red River.

On June 26 off Greenland they saw their first icebergs, a cold and ominous sight. The icebergs and floes continued about them, growing more numerous and menacing as the ship headed toward Resolution Island at the mouth of Hudson Strait. The realization of how far north they had come dismayed some of the colonists. Captain von May, one of the settlers wrote in later years, had assured them that the climate where they were going was "perfect, maturing all kinds of grain and fruits."[18] Now they were not so sure whether von May had told them the truth.

From time to time since they had embarked at Dordrecht, young Peter had busied himself sketching incidents of the trip. The frigid scenes of the northern waters provided exciting new subjects for his pencil, and on June 26 he began to record detailed, carefully drawn views of the *Wellington* amid the ice.[19] During the night of June 29 a drifting iceberg hit the *Wellington*, and he depicted that scene. The next day the floes and icebergs were thick around the ship, and Peter sketched a view of the colonists getting off the *Wellington* to walk and frolic on the ice.

On July 14, still pushing past expansive floes and towering icebergs, the ship reached the vicinity of Resolution Island off the Labrador coast and was forced to halt temporarily and set its anchor in the pack ice alongside the vessel. Two other ships, similarly halted, were sitting nearby. They were the Hudson's Bay Company's ships *Prince of Wales* and *Eddystone,* carrying supplies and Indian trade goods to York Factory, and waiting to guide the *Wellington* into Hudson Bay. On the evening of July 15 two other vessels also came in view, H.M.S. *Hecla* and H.M.S. *Fury,* British naval ships, bound under the command of Captain William Edward Parry on an exploring expedition in search of a Northwest Passage.

Despite the unpleasant situation of the Swiss colonists aboard the *Wellington,* they seem to have been making the best of it and not allowing the presence of danger to undermine their morale. As the *Hecla* drew near them in the early evening, Captain George Francis Lyon, an officer aboard Parry's ship, noted strange activity aboard the *Wellington.* "We observed the settlers waltzing on deck for above two hours," he wrote in his journal soon afterward, when he had discovered who the *Wellington's* passengers were, "the men in old-fashioned grey jackets and the women wearing long-eared mobcaps, like those used by the Swiss peasants. . . . The Dutchmen [*sic*]," he went on, after referring to the nineteen days that the *Wellington* had been among the icebergs, "had, however, behaved very philosophically during this period, and seemed determined on being merry, in spite of the weather. Several marriages had taken place (the surgeon, who was accompanying them to their colony, acting as parson) and many more were in agitation; each happy couple always deferring the ceremony until a fine day allowed of an evening's ball, which was only terminated by a fresh breeze or a fall of snow."[20]

On July 16 the ships moved slowly forward and came abreast of Resolution Island, where young Peter sighted walruses and polar bears and drew sketches of them. The next night the *Hecla* and *Fury* drifted more than two miles ahead of the other ships and were soon out of sight. The *Wellington* proceeded ahead with its two escort vessels, and on July 21 Peter recorded the scene when a collision between the *Wellington* and *Eddystone* broke spars on each ship. Resolution Island had been uninhabited, but on July 23 the three vessels moved close to the Labrador coast, and numerous seal-hunting Eskimos came through the open water lanes in kayaks to press around the ships. The Hudson's Bay Company men fired guns on the ships to impress the Eskimos, but a number of the natives forced their way aboard the *Wellington*. The meeting was a friendly one, and some of the colonists even went ashore to visit the Eskimos' settlement. There, according to the later recollection of one of the colonists, Dr. Louis Jacques Ostertag of the emigrant party treated the Eskimos for some complaint. The brief halt provided Peter with opportunities to make the first of his many depictions of native peoples of the New World, and it is evident that he was among those who went ashore on the rocky coast, where he drew detailed sketches of Eskimo families.

Shortly afterward the ships moved on, groping for the entrance to Hudson Bay. On July 24 disaster almost overtook them. During the night the *Prince of Wales* ran onto an iceberg, which by dawn had stove in the ship's bulwarks. One of Peter's drawings depicts the scene, showing the *Prince of Wales* atilt, leaning against the iceberg it had rammed, and members of its crew scrambling across the ice to the *Eddystone*. Part of the *Prince of Wales'* cargo was transferred to the *Wellington*, and the damaged ship was repaired. The next day, in foggy and rainy weather, the *Wellington* was in trouble. It, too, smashed against an iceberg and for a while was in danger of being crushed in the ice. Peter's sketch of that tense scene, showing people getting off the *Wellington* to examine the vessel's side, bore his notation, written, as he usually did, in German, that the colonists were then at "Lat. 61. 42 N."

All the ships eventually got underway again and, in time, broke through the ice and made their way safely into the less dangerous waters of Hudson Bay. On August 17 they came in sight of the tall flagpole and buildings of York Factory on a bluff above the bay, and after they had anchored, Peter drew a view of the scene, as dinghies ferried the colonists and their baggage ashore. The voyage had taken 79 days, and even though the settlers were in a bleak and formidable-looking northern country, still far from their ultimate destination, they must have been happy and relieved to set foot once again on firm ground.

They remained at the fur post only long enough for the Hudson's Bay Company authorities to organize the expedition that would take them inland to Red River. While the Swiss families recuperated from the sea trip and prepared for the second leg of their journey, Peter continued to find new and wondrous scenes to depict around the post. What was probably his first sketch of an American Indian group was made at this time. It was a vigorous drawing of a tall, long-haired Cree Indian hunter and his wife and children. The Indian family had apparently just arrived at the British post, and the hunter is portrayed with his gun and several dead ducks.[21]

Also present at the post was the Reverend John West, a Church of England clergyman, who in 1820 had been sent from England by the Hudson's Bay Company to serve as chaplain at the Red River settlement. West had established himself at Red River, conducting services for the colonists already there. He also traveled extensively to other company forts to administer to traders and employees and to preach to the Indians, and now he had come to York Factory to help welcome the new colonists and aid them on the difficult journey inland to Red River. While the families waited, he married several Swiss couples and baptized six children who had been born during the voyage from Europe.

The colonists finally departed for the interior in two groups, the first party leaving York Factory about a week after their arrival, and the second group, which included the Rindisbachers and the Reverend West, some two weeks later, on September 6. The families traveled in big York boats, which the company employed on the rivers and lakes of the interior of the continent. There were only enough craft available to carry the passengers; a large part of their baggage had to be left behind, a misfortune that added to their hardships during their first winter at Red River.

The York boats, propelled by fur company oarsmen, but also able to hoist sails when conditions favored their use, took them up the Hayes

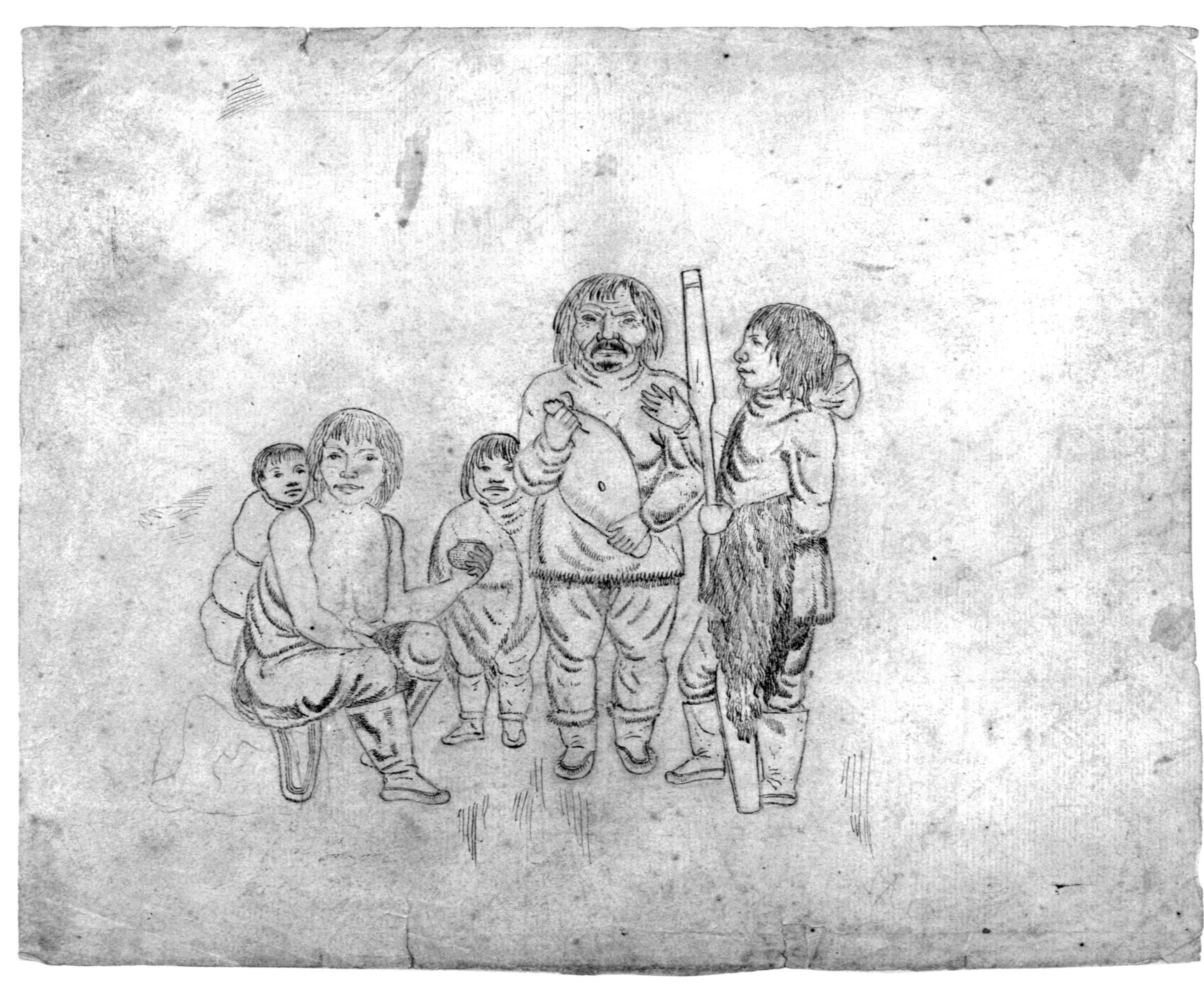

VII. An Eskimo family [Untitled].
Pen and ink, 7½ x 9⅛ inches, ca. 1821.
Courtesy of Mrs. Frances Rindesbacher Eustice, Cleveland Heights, Ohio.

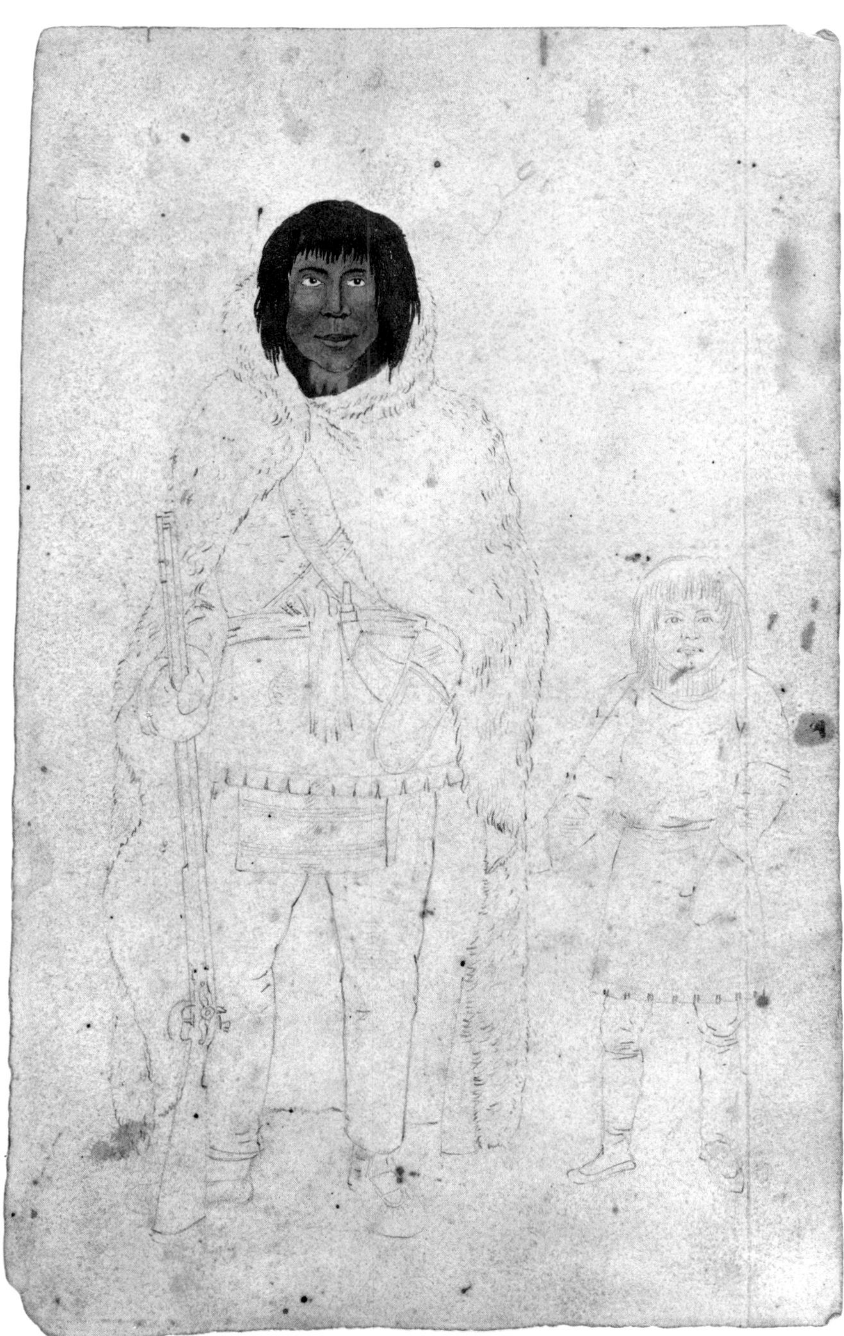

VIII. An Eskimo and child [Untitled].
Pencil and watercolor, 9⅛ x 5⅝ inches, ca. 1822/1823.
Courtesy of Mrs. Frances Rindesbacher Eustice, Cleveland Heights, Ohio.

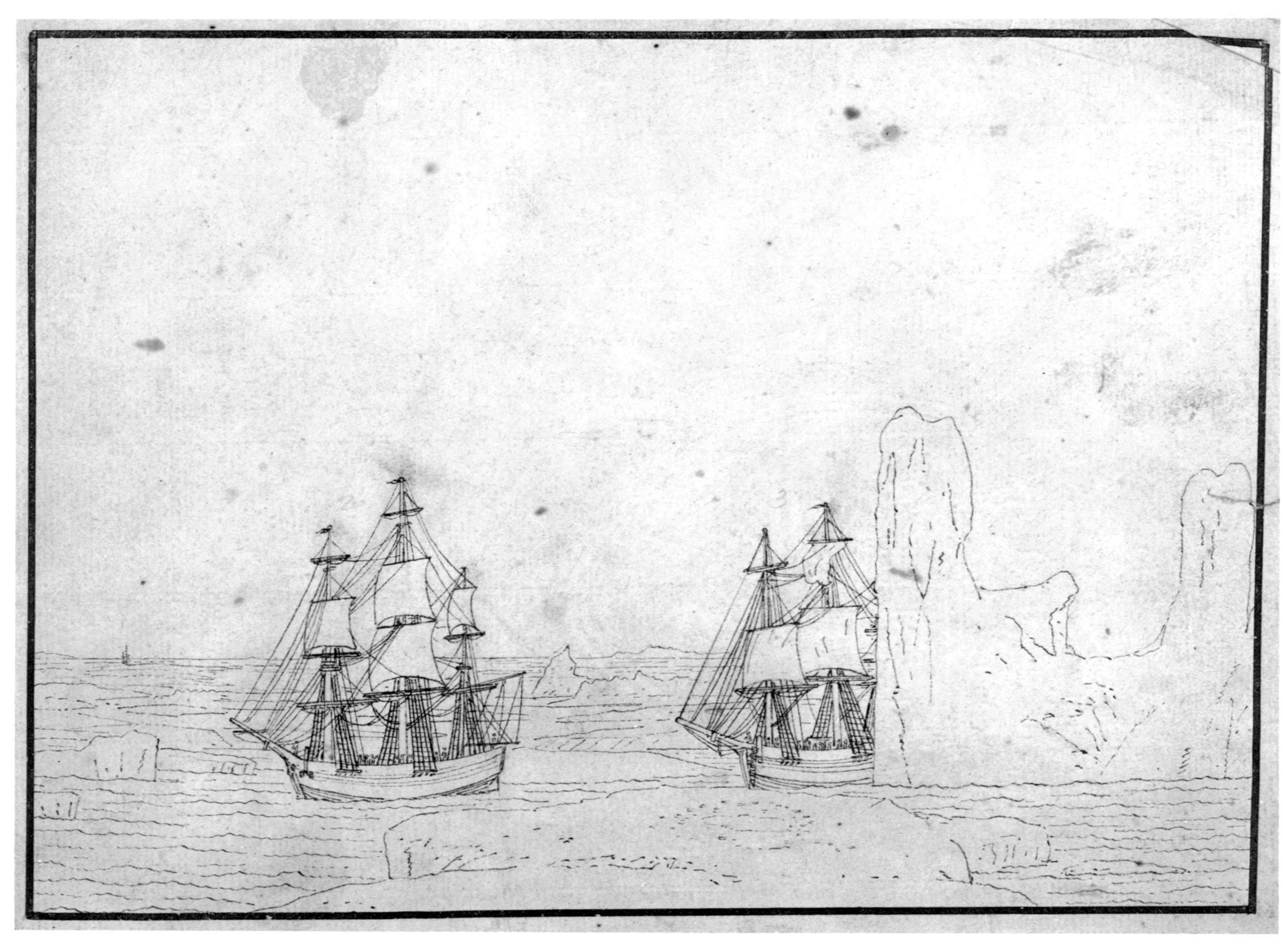

IX. The *Wellington* in danger of being crushed by an iceberg [Untitled].
Pen and ink, 7⅜ x 9½ inches, 1821.
Courtesy of Mrs. Frances Rindesbacher Eustice, Cleveland Heights, Ohio.

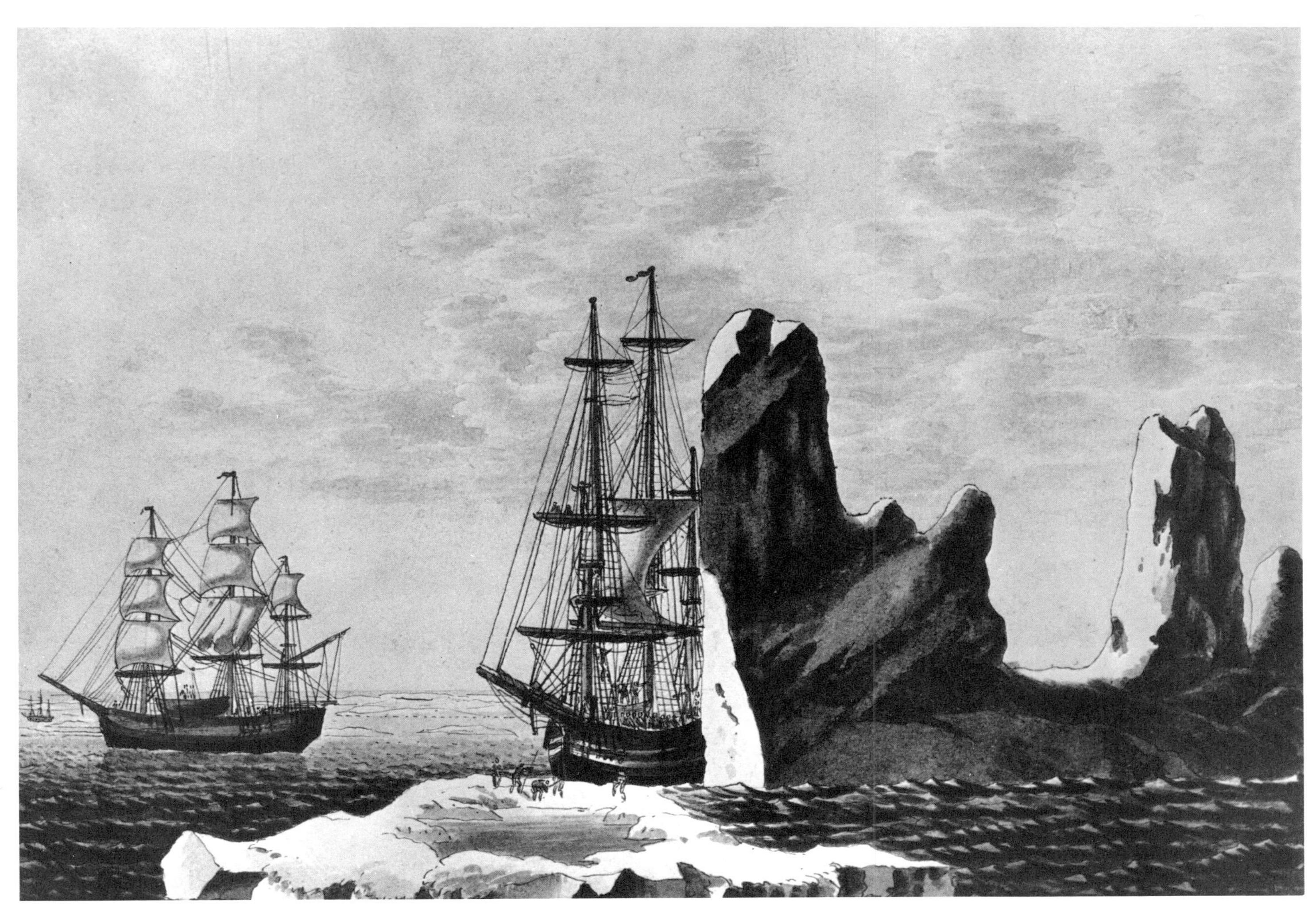

X. *Great Danger of the Ship* Wellington *of Being Crushed by an Iceberg at Lat. 61.42 N, July 25, 1821.*
Finished watercolor after the ink drawing (left), 6¼ x 8⅝ inches, ca. 1821.
Courtesy of the Public Archives of Canada, Ottawa.

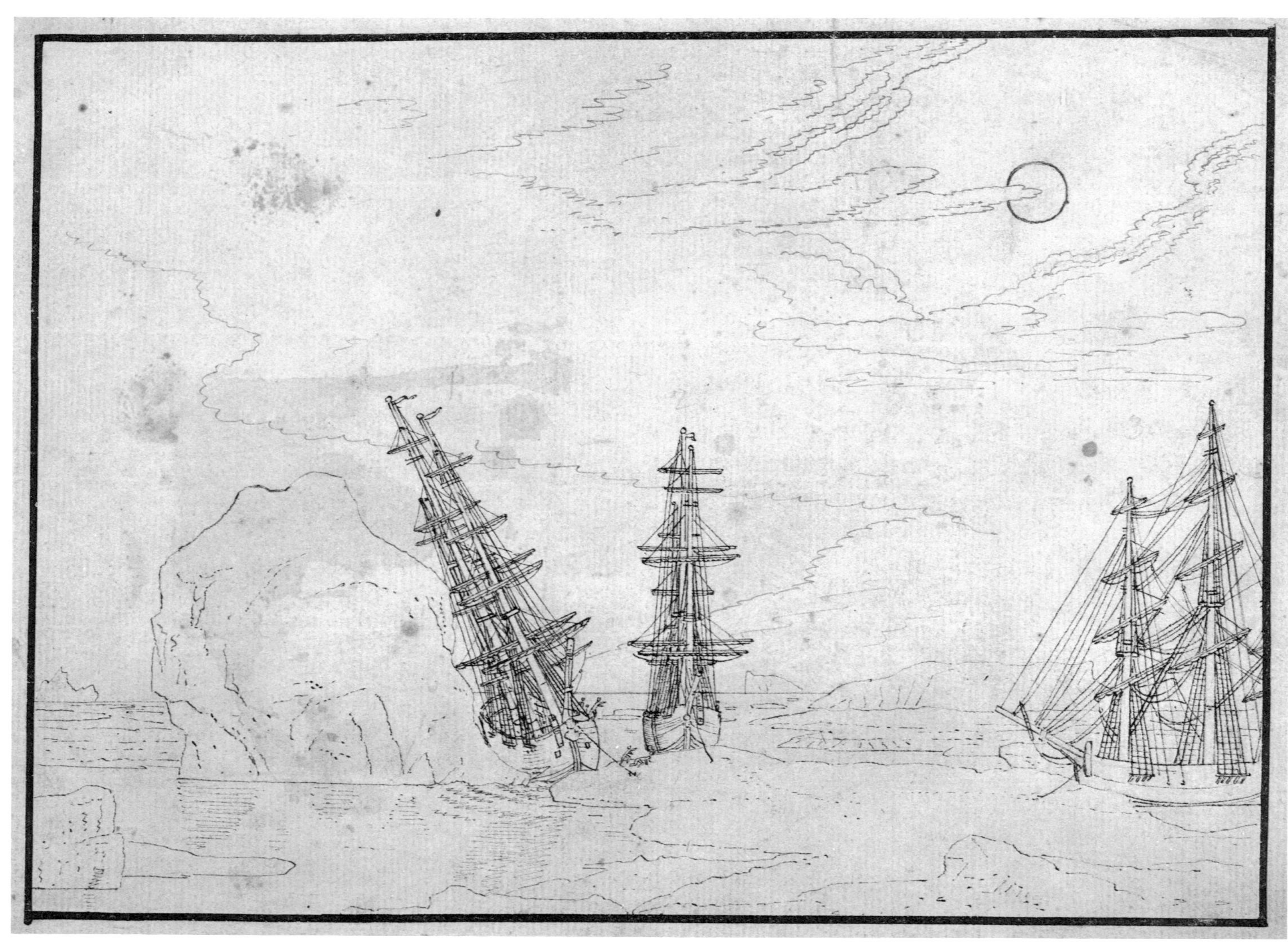

XI. The *Prince of Wales* stuck fast on an iceberg [Untitled].
Pen and ink, 7⅜ x 9⁷⁄₁₆ inches, ca. 1821.
Courtesy of Mrs. Frances Rindesbacher Eustice, Cleveland Heights, Ohio.

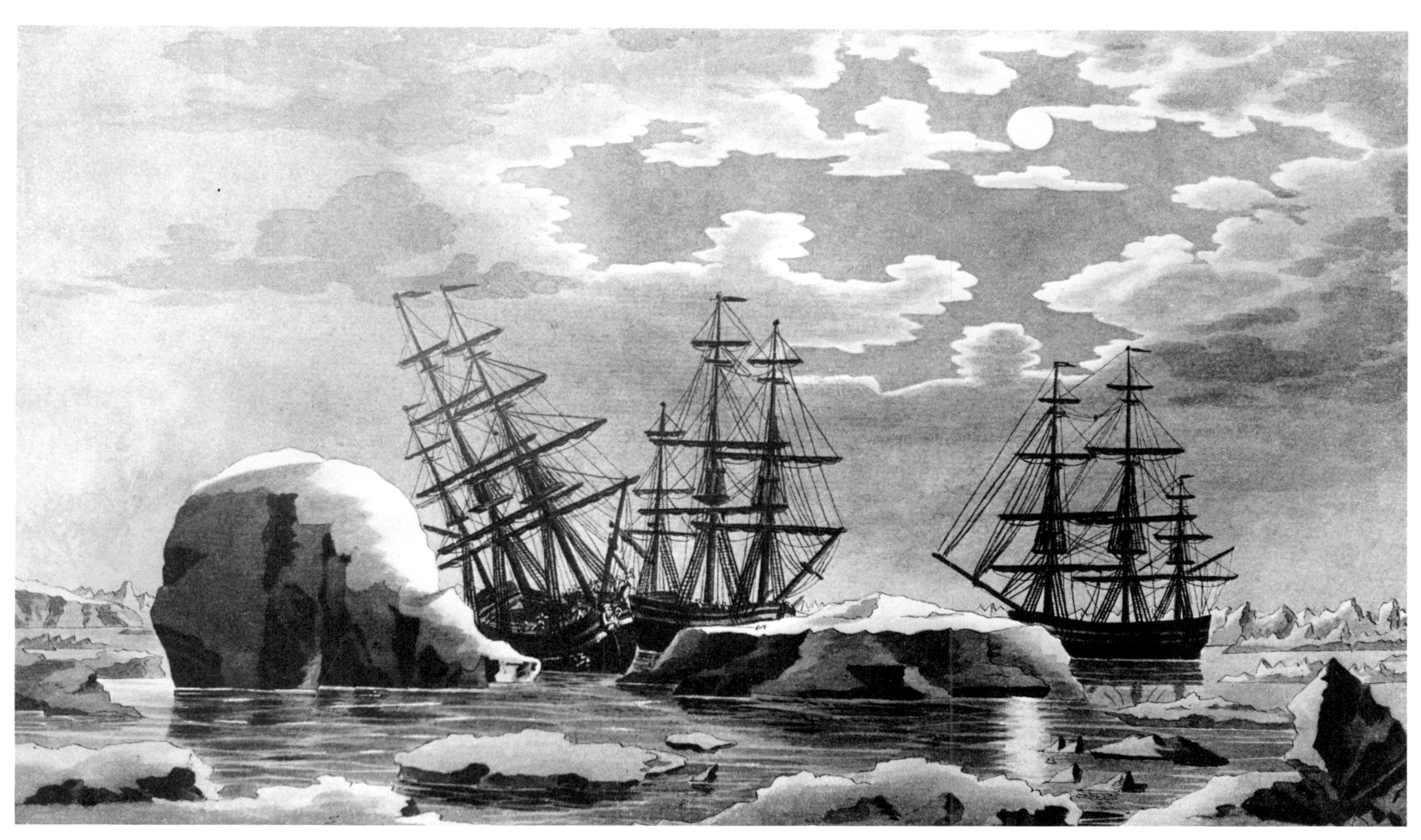

XII. *The Ship* **Prince of Wales** *Runs Aground on an Iceberg During the Night of July 24, 1821. Lat. 61.42 N Long. 65.12 W.*
Finished pen and ink wash after the ink drawing (left), 8½ x 12½ inches, ca. 1821.
Courtesy of the Public Archives of Canada, Ottawa.

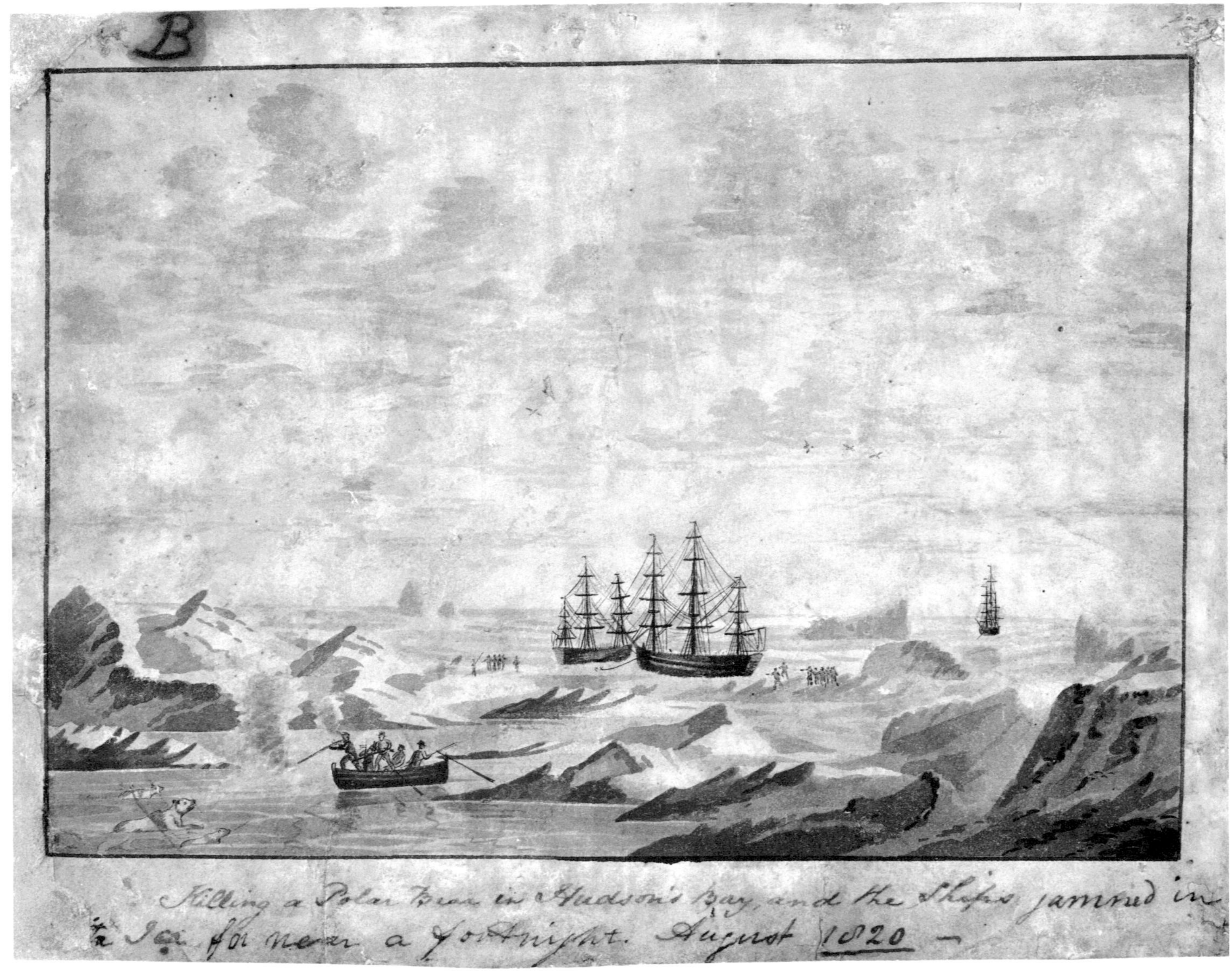

**XIII. *Killing a Polar Bear in Hudson's Bay, and the Ship Jammed
into the Ice for Near a Fortnight, August, 1820.***
In this drawing Rindisbacher was probably depicting a scene for someone
who had encountered similar hardships and adventures while journeying
to America and who wanted to retain a pictorial record of that experience.
Pen and ink wash, 5¹³⁄₁₆ x 8¹⁄₁₆ inches, ca. 1821/1823.
Collection of Amon Carter Museum, Fort Worth.

River and its tributary, the Hill, to Lake Winnipeg. It was a long, gruelling trip through the wilds, full of many dangers and discomforts. In numerous places the rivers were so shallow at that time of year that the colonists had to get out and walk along the wooded shore while the straining crews poled, pushed or pulled the craft over the rocky bottom. At other times, difficult portages had to be made around waterfalls or perilous rapids. On occasion, the travelers perhaps passed Indians, for one of Peter's watercolors, which he made later in his life, shows a group of natives portaging around Trout Falls on the Hayes River, a scene he would have witnessed only during the trip to Red River in 1821.

When the emigrants reached Lake Winnipeg on October 11, their distress increased. The weather turned cold and stormy, and the boats' progress along the lake's long western shore, often in driving rain and against headwinds, was slow and miserable. On October 23 one of the York boats was wrecked on a rock. It caused a delay to the entire party, whose members had to camp for a week on the lake's wild shore, huddled around fires against the rain and cold, and feeling hunger also because they had nothing to eat but "grain" and a few fish that they were able to catch.[22] By November 1, when the group that included the Rindisbachers reached the mouth of Red River at the southern end of the lake, one man had drowned and six children had died ("only" one man, and "only" six children, the Reverend John West noted in his diary, as if, in view of the many hardships of the trip, it were truly amazing).

On the way, Peter had sketched many of the memorable scenes, and these pictures, forming a unique documentary record of the inland trip, are the only illustrations known today that show what it was like to travel that much-used Canadian fur route from Hudson Bay to Red River at that early date. His vivid, detailed drawings, some of them originals made on the scene and others watercolor copies that he executed at later times, include not only views of the York boats on the Hayes and Hill rivers and on Lake Winnipeg, and moments of pulling over shallows and portaging around rapids, but also depictions, now historically important, of the Hudson's Bay Company's inland fur posts, including Rock Fort, Fort Logan, and Oxford House on the rivers and the famed Norway House at the head of Lake Winnipeg, all of which the colonists passed during the trip.

At the mouth of Red River, the weary and hungry travelers came on an encampment of Chippewa Indians, headed by an old friend of the Hudson's Bay Company named Peguis.[23] In 1800, when Peguis was 26 years old, he had led his band from its homeland on Lake Superior to Red River to be closer to the British traders, and from the first days of

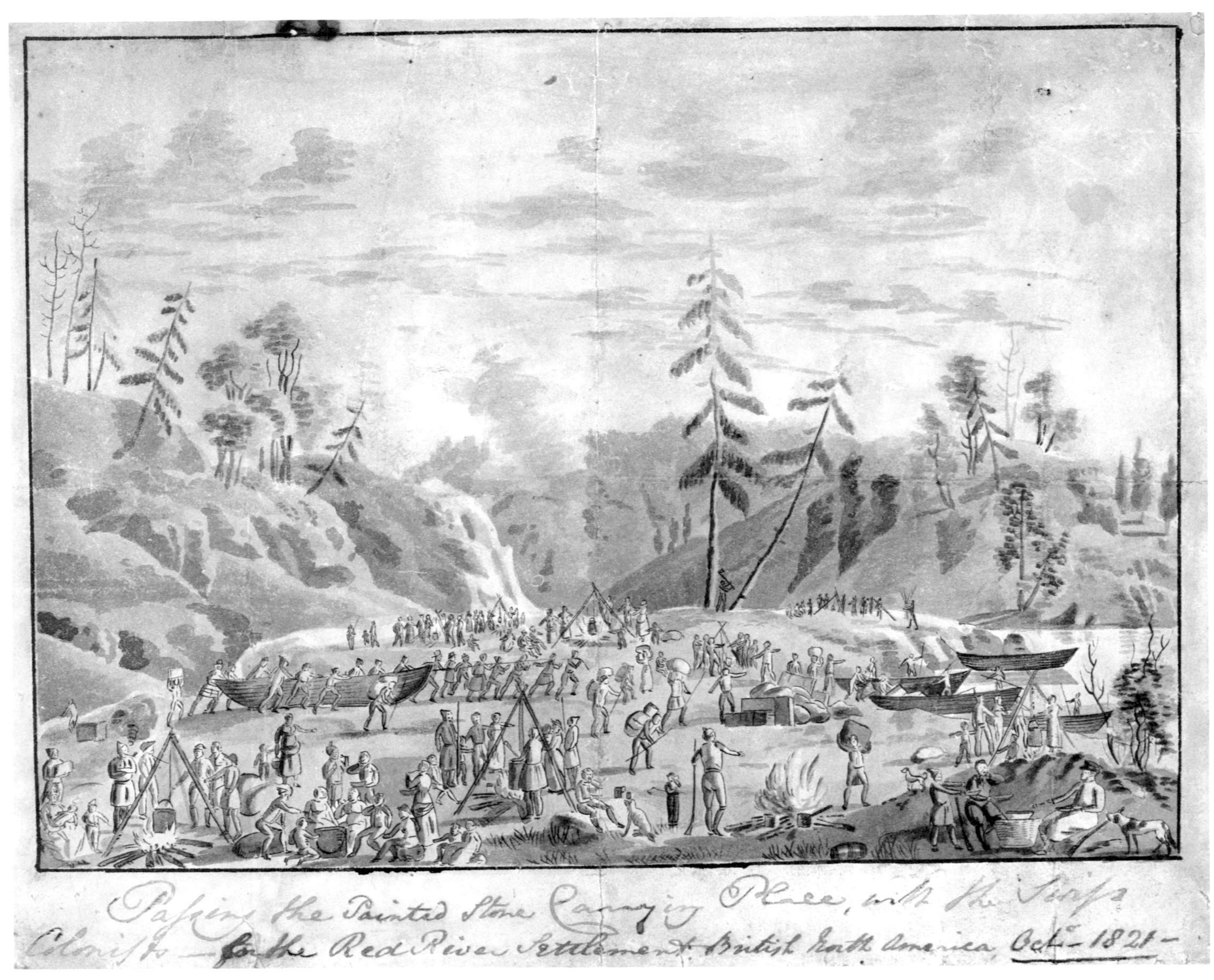

**XIV. *Taking the Painted Stone Carrying Place, with the Swiss Colonists
for the Red River Settlement, British North America, October, 1821.***
Pen and ink wash, 6¹⁄₁₆ x 8 inches, ca. 1821/1823.
Collection of Amon Carter Museum, Fort Worth.

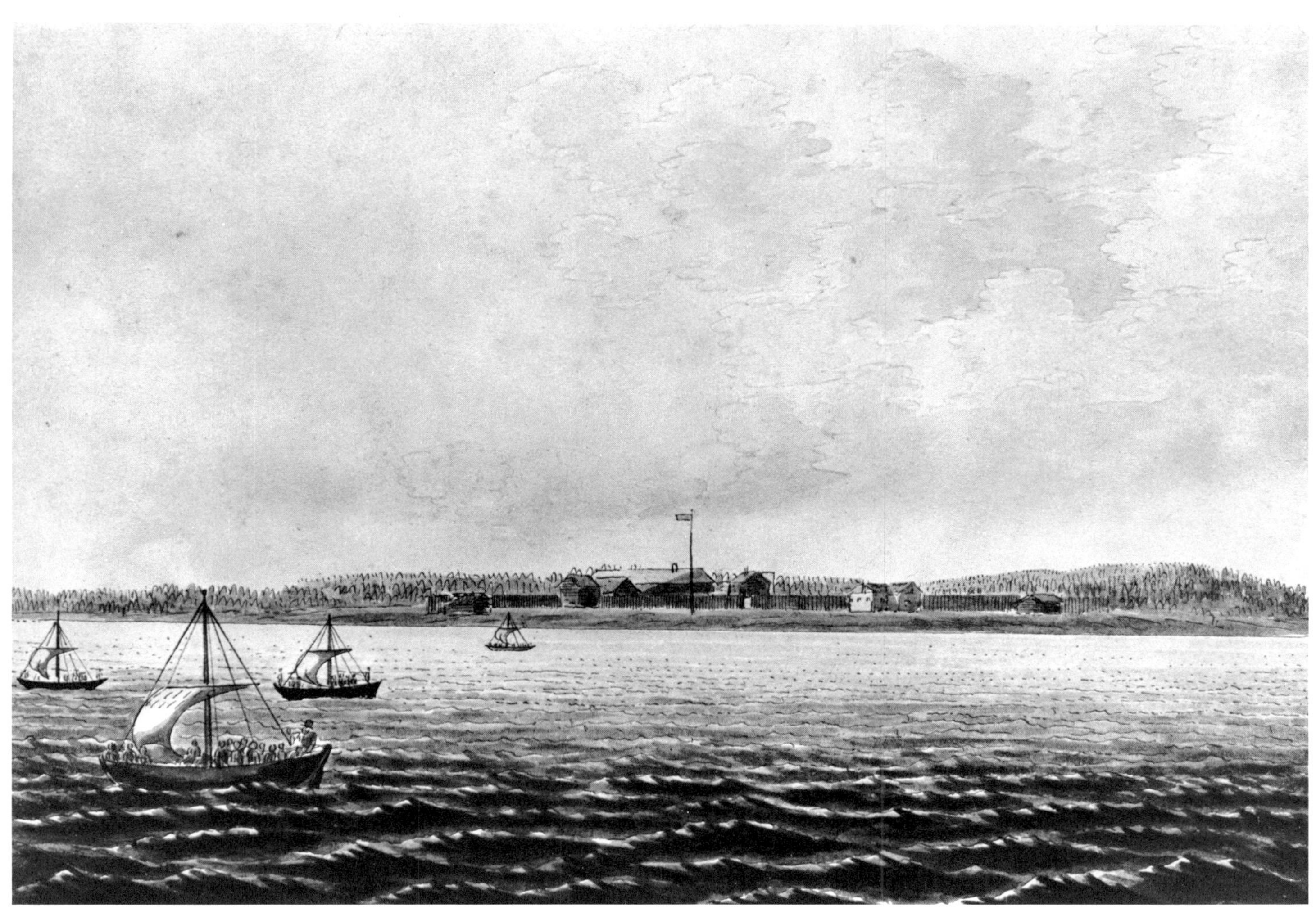

**XV. *Arrival at Norway House on the Great Lake Winipesi, Oct. 14,
and Departures Thence, Oct. 16, 1821.***
Watercolor, 6¼ x 8⅝ inches, ca. 1821.
Courtesy of the Public Archives of Canada, Ottawa.

the Selkirk colony he and his people had befriended the settlers. In 1817 Lord Selkirk had given him a silver medal and a signed parchment in recognition of the help he had provided the struggling colony. Now, again, he showed his warm friendship for the whites by welcoming the large company of famished Swiss travelers into his camp and giving them, said the Reverend West, "a good supply of fresh and dried sturgeon." When West returnd to England in 1823, he took with him five paintings which Rindisbacher had made. They included two of Peter's Eskimo scenes, a view of a buffalo and of an Indian family, and a full length portrait of an Indian holding a gun and a knife tomahawk, with a bow and arrows slung at his back. The latter painting may be of Peguis, drawn when the colonists first met him, though the Indian wears a large triangular belled object (a looking glass?) around his neck, rather than — as might be supposed — the silver medal that Selkirk had given him.

The colonists proceeded about thirty-five miles up the Red River to Fort Douglas, the seat of the colony's government, where they were welcomed by the Governor, Alexander Macdonell. Other than Macdonell's compassionate greetings, however, nothing but bad news awaited them. The homes and farmsteads of the earlier colonists lay on the prairie about Fort Douglas, but during the preceding summer grasshoppers had destroyed almost all their crops, and the newcomers were literally facing a winter of starvation in their new homeland. The cold weather was already upon them, and emergency measures had to be considered at once.[24] What supplies they had brought upriver from York Factory with them were far from sufficient for so many people for the winter, and after tense discussions it was decided to send some seventy-five of the hardiest of the new arrivals farther up the Red River to a small Hudson's Bay Company post at Pembina, which lay in buffalo country near the present-day border between Canada and the United States. There, where it was believed that buffalo, deer and elk would be more abundant, and where the whites could trade with Indians for pemmican and dried meat, the winter could be passed, and in the spring the party could return to the others at Fort Douglas and establish their new homes.

The colonists were disheartened and angry, and many of them now blamed Captain von May for having misled them. Some of them protested that they had understood that they had been bound for the Red River of Louisiana, much farther south, where other French-speaking inhabitants dwelled and where the climate was actually what had been represented to them. Macdonell could do nothing to help them, however, and there was little time for recriminations. The southward-bound party left Fort Douglas and reached Pembina just in time to erect huts and gather wood for fuel before winter closed in.

One group of five Swiss families went even farther south. Earlier in the fall, a band of armed Americans, carrying out a contract made previously with Lord Selkirk, had driven a herd of cattle almost 1,500 miles from Missouri to Red River for the use of the Colony.[25] In November the drovers set off to return home, and the five Swiss families, deciding to abandon Red River and seek a milder climate farther south, went with them as far as Fort St. Anthony, an American military post built in 1819 at the confluence of the St. Peter's (Minnesota) and Mississippi rivers near present-day Minneapolis and St. Paul. The Swiss remained in abandoned barracks at the fort during the winter, and in the spring built cabins for themselves on the military reservation near the fort, raising crops to sell to the garrison (the Fifth United States Infantry under Colonel Josiah Snelling), and becoming the first permanent white settlers in the present state of Minnesota.

The Rindisbachers, it seems probable, remained during the winter in the home of one of the earlier colonists in the vicinity of Fort Douglas. Both there and at Pembina, however, it was a cold, desperate winter, and supplies ran short. At the fort, the settlers depended mostly on meager rations of roots and wheat given to them by the fur company, supplemented by meat brought in by hunting bands of Indians and by fish which the colonists caught through holes cut in the river ice. On a bluff above the junction of the Red and Assiniboine rivers near Fort Douglas stood Fort Gibraltar, an old North West Company fur post which the Hudson's Bay Company had acquired and was rebuilding, and in December, 1821, one month after he had arrived at Red River, Peter drew a lively scene of the settlers and friendly Indians of the vicinity on the ice below Fort Gibraltar, showing some of the people busily trying to catch fish through holes in the ice.

At Pembina, which Peter may also have visited during his first winter on Red River, the settlers fought off starvation by buying buffalo meat from any Indians who showed up, by fishing through the ice, and by going onto the snowy plains with dogs and sleds obtained from the Indians and trying to hunt buffalo themselves. Those ventures met with little success, for the buffalo were scarce, and the settlers were inexperienced. Some of the newly-arrived colonists, one of them later wrote, were maimed for life when their hands and feet froze on the plains.[26] By spring, many of the settlers had eaten dog and horse meat to stay alive, and as the weather warmed and the snow melted, they varied their diet further with such edibles as acorns and the seed-balls of wild roses, which the women gathered and cooked with a little buffalo fat.

Soon after May 1, the colonists were again united at Fort Douglas. George Simpson, the Hudson's Bay Company's Governor, visited the Colony and was appalled by what he heard and saw. "Your Agent, Captn. Du May has certainly not done his duty conscientiously," he wrote to Andrew Colvile, a director of the company in England, noting further that the pamphlets distributed to the colonists in Switzerland had been "highly colored" and that the settlers had been led to expect of the Red River country "more than can be realized."[27]

"Little or no provision has been made for them here," Simpson went on in his letter to Colvile, under date of May 20, 1822, "indeed the crops were so unproductive, and the Provision Trade during the summer [of 1821] so triffling, that nothing of consequence could be collected, and the unprecedented and almost total failure of the Buffalo with the encreased population, has made this Colony the most distressing scene of starvation that can well be conceived. I have not heard that any persons connected with the Settlement have actually perished through hunger, but soul and body have been kept together on next to nothing, chiefly by a little musty Grain which Mr. McDonell served out with great economy and an esculent root called 'Indian Potatoes' resembling a horse raddish in appearance but very insipid; this root which is plentiful here they eat either raw or boiled, but possesses little nourishment....

"On their arrival Mr. McDonell sent the greater part of them to Pambina for the purpose of being near the Buffalo, where they chiefly remained until the opening of the navigation; they did through Freemen and Indians pick up a triffling supply of animal food, but how they have spun out the Winter and Spring is unexplicable; Horses, Dogs, Bears, Buffalo in short whatever came in their way was devoured."[28]

Despite their hardships during the winter, however, the settlers at both places had managed to keep up their spirits. The Swiss veterans of the de Meuron regiment had welcomed the newcomers from their home country and had tried to make them comfortable. Some of the bachelors among the veterans had been particularly pleased by the appearance of marriageable daughters among the newly-arrived families, and a number of weddings had occurred, linking not only the veterans to the new families, but one emigrant family to another. There were parties and dances, with fiddlers playing popular Swiss airs, and wedding cakes made from coarse flour ground from wheat in the settlers' small rotary coffee mills, to which were added buffalo fat and salt. There were also births; another son, Frederic, was born to the Rindisbachers.[29]

With the coming of good weather, the families began to erect homes on the lands allotted to them near the confluence of the Red and Assiniboine rivers.[30] The cattle that had been driven up from Missouri the previous fall was distributed to them, but despite the promises that von May had given them in Switzerland, no seeds or farming implements had been sent across the Atlantic Ocean for them, and they had to use spades and hoes instead of plows, and procure what seeds they could from the older, established colonists. In spite of their difficulties, however, they managed to raise enough food that year to see them through the following winter.

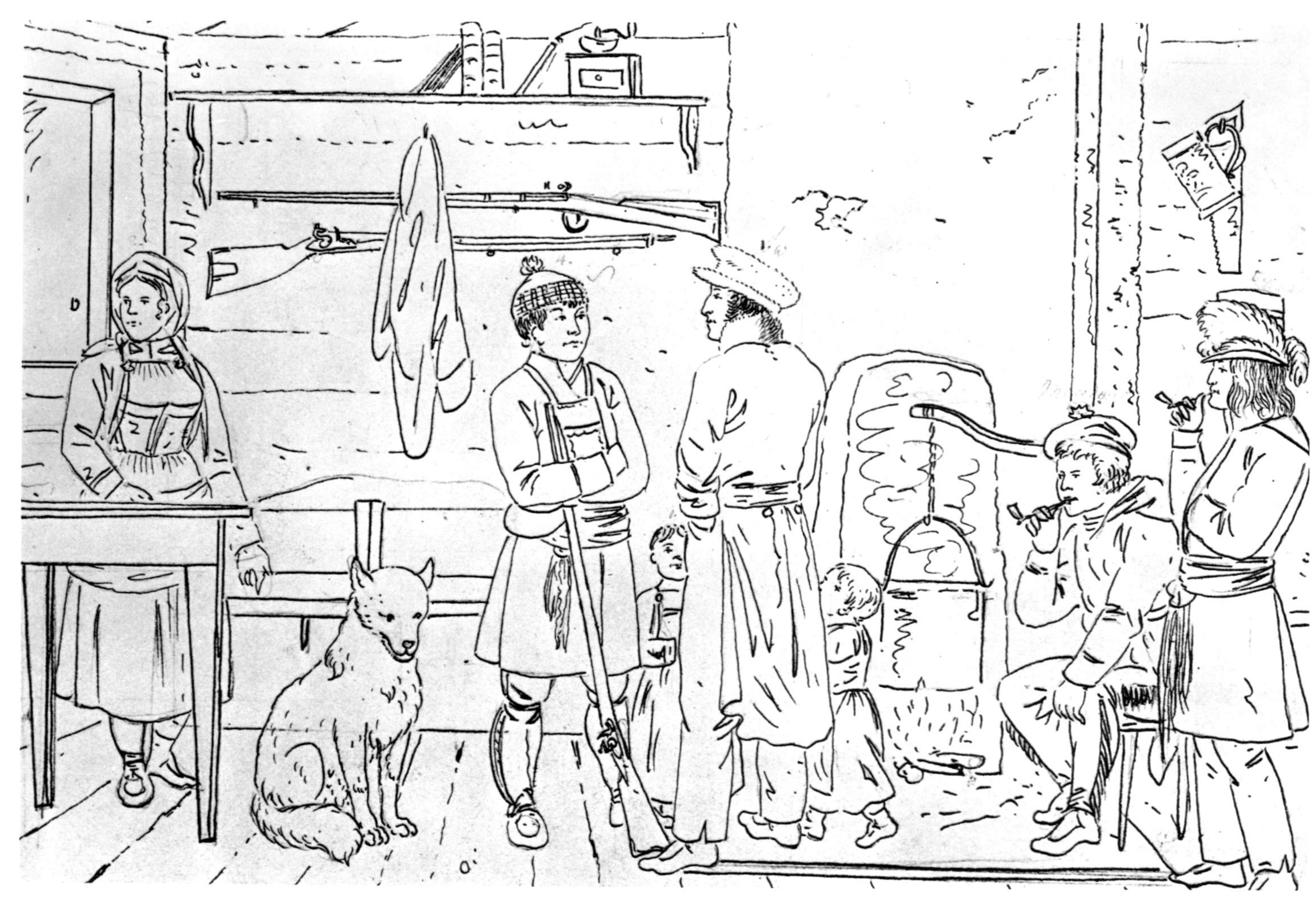

XVI. *Colonists on the Red River in North America.*
The artist was probably depicting his family in the company of some friends. The faint numbers penciled in above the figures perhaps corresponded with a list of names. It is possible that the woman on the left is Peter's mother and that Peter and his father stand conversing in the center of the picture while his sister, Verena and the adopted child, Gautier, look up at their father.
Pen and ink, 5⅜ x 6⅜ inches, ca. 1825.
Courtesy of the Public Archives of Canada, Ottawa.

III. AT RED RIVER

The Rindisbachers got their home finished in 1822, and there, along the Red River, for almost five years, they tried to make a go of it. The violence of the Colony's immediate past was ended, but there were constant frustrations and disillusionments. In April, 1822, the Hudson's Bay Company fur men moved into the rehabilitated Fort Gibraltar at the forks of the Red and Assiniboine rivers and renamed it Fort Garry. The Colony's store was moved from Fort Douglas, the Colony's headquarters building, to Fort Garry, and the settlers were able to draw upon that new post for certain of their supplies.[31] But again and again the Colony faced famine. There were crop failures and short crops, grasshoppers and ruinous prairie fires. Whenever meat was needed, it seemed that buffalo were scarce or non-existent on the nearby plains. Still, the Rindisbacher family held on in their new home.[32]

During those years, as Peter grew to manhood, he continued to sketch and paint, using pencil, pen, and watercolors, and drawing principally on the colorful Indian life around him for subjects. Various groups of Chippewas, Crees, Assiniboines, and Eastern Sioux frequented the British fur posts, trading pelts, meat and pemmican for white men's goods and alcohol. The Sioux, who came up from Minnesota, were traditional enemies of the other tribes, and their appearance was sometimes the signal for trouble. One Sioux band in particular, that led by the well-known Yanktonai, Waneta, who had helped the British in the War of 1812 and had gained the name "The Charger" because of his reckless bravery in attacking the Americans at Fort Meigs and Sandusky, resented the incursions of the Métis and Crees, Chippewas, and Assiniboines into Sioux hunting grounds near Pembina. In May, 1822, Waneta and his Sioux warriors threw the whites and halfbloods at Pembina into a panic when they almost wiped out two nearby camps of Chippewas

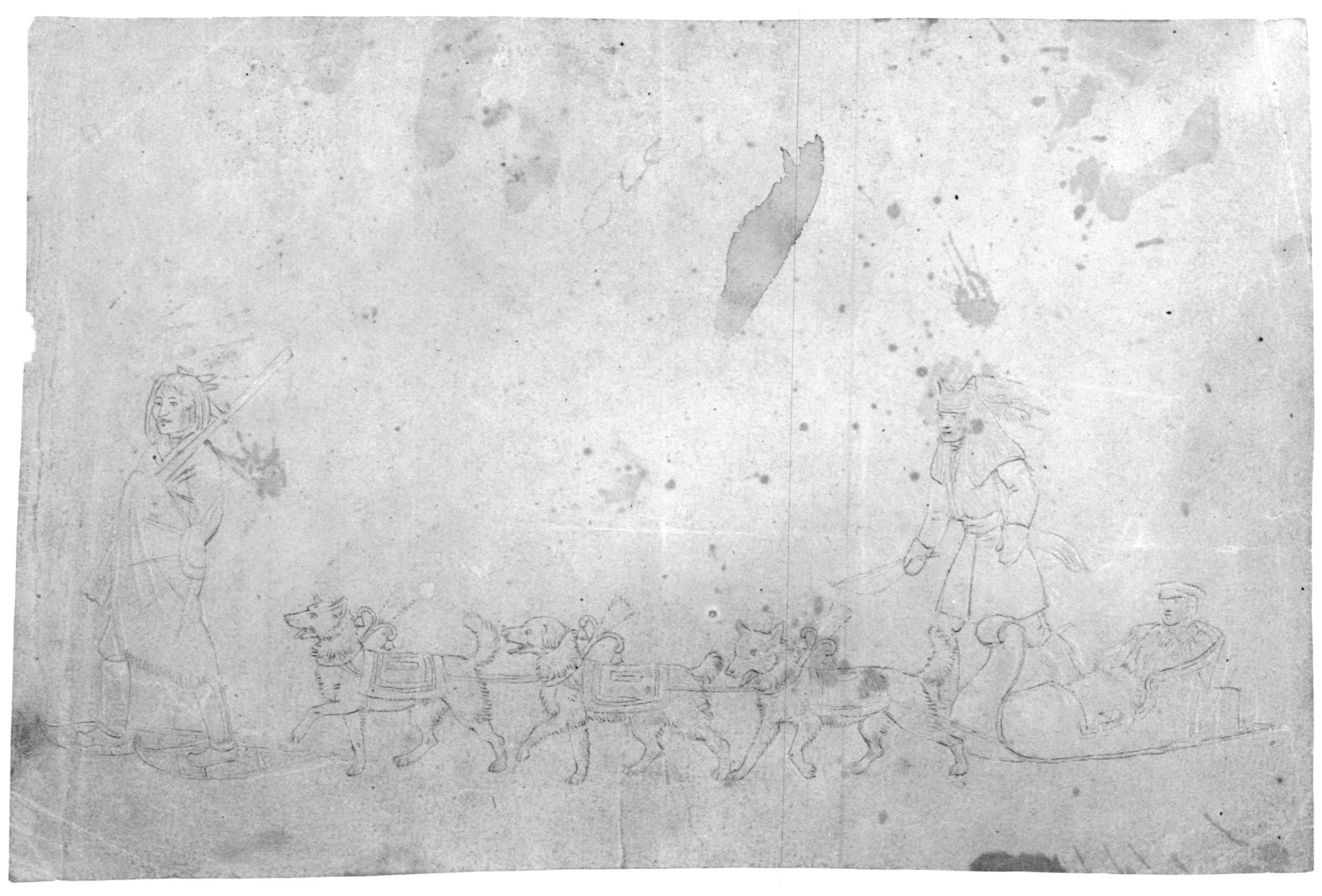

XVII. Winter voyaging in a light sledge [Untitled].
A preliminary sketch for the watercolor (right).
Pencil, 6½ x 9½ inches, ca. 1822/1823.
Courtesy of Mrs. Frances Rindesbacher Eustice, Cleveland Heights, Ohio.

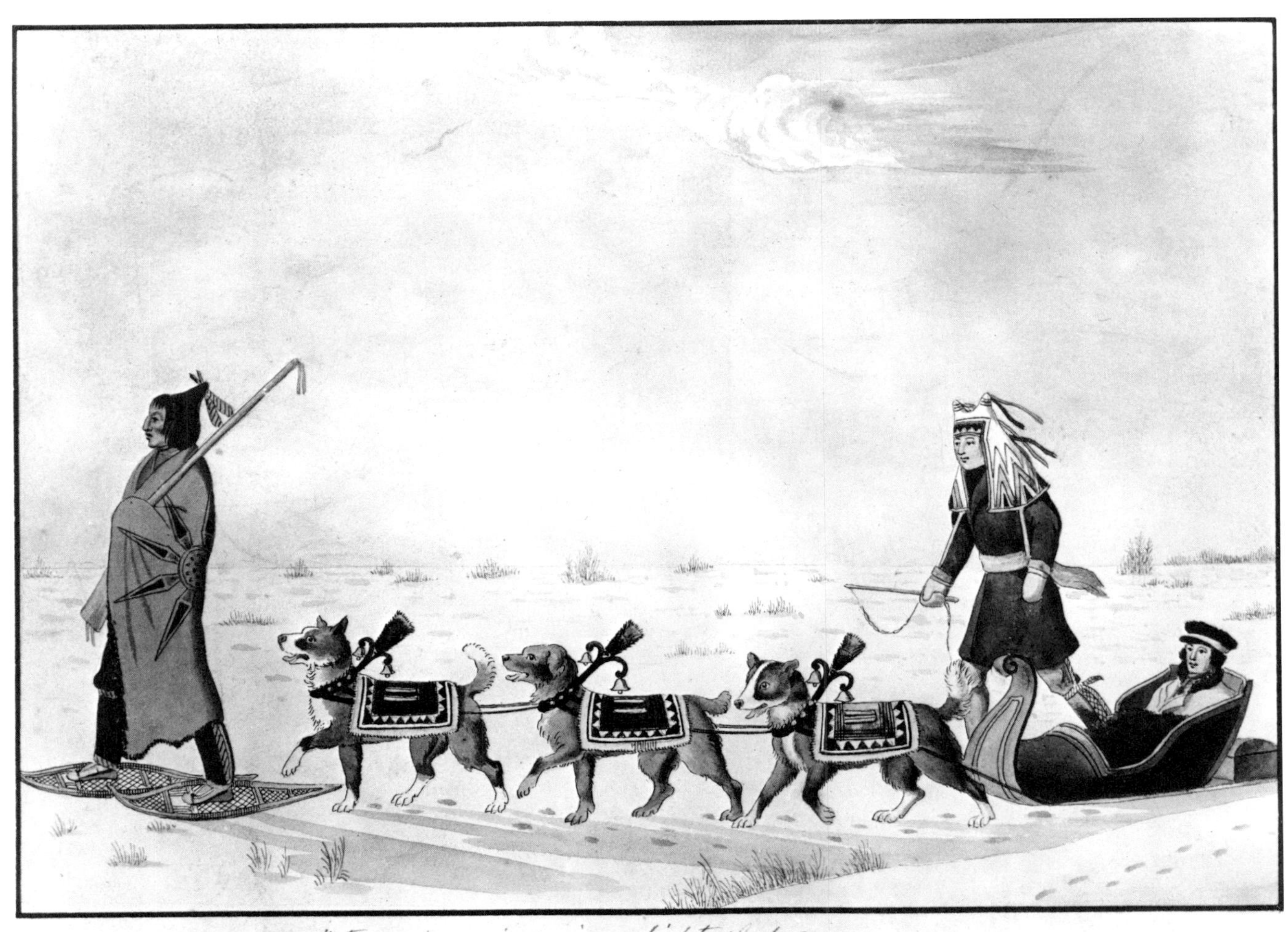

XVIII. *Winter Voyaging in a Light Sledge.*
Watercolor, 6⅞ x 9¼ inches, ca. 1822/1823.
Courtesy of M. Knoedler and Co., Inc., New York.

and Assiniboines. For a while, Pembina itself was threatened. Governor Simpson hurried to the scene, and despite his anger at some of the settlers who had decided "to sneak for safety to Lake Winnipeg," rallied a group of Métis and about thirty de Meurons and twenty other volunteers and organized a defense.[33] The Sioux threat soon evaporated, and Waneta made peace with the peppery little Hudson's Bay Company official. Although there is no proof of it, Peter may well have been at Pembina during the time, for he drew a view of the two company posts "on the level prairie at Pembina on the Red River, and surprise by the savages at nightfall of May 25, 1822," and also a painting of Waneta, which he noted was "Drawn from nature."

Whether or not he had been a participant in that episode with the Sioux, Peter had almost daily opportunities to depict colorful aspects of Indian life. Summer and winter, he observed different groups of Indians as they traveled across the neighboring prairies or paddled on the rivers. He became friends with some of the Indians and Métis and was welcomed in their camps. He visited the villages of barkcovered lodges of woodland-dwelling Chippewas and the buffalo-skin tipis of the Crees and Assiniboines of the plains and was the first artist known to depict the interior of a Plains Indian tipi. He drew the Indians fishing, hunting, and engaging in drunken orgies on the ferocious trade alcohol that the fur men gave them. At the same time, he caught the full flavor of the Red River Colony of the period, recording, along with Indian life, views of the Métis and British traders around the forts and of the Swiss and Scottish settlers, as well as scenes of the buildings and countryside of the Colony. The details of his sketches and paintings were often so accurate and complete that today historians and students of Indian life and of the Red River Colony and trade center scrutinize them carefully for what they reveal. In his works, for example, may be observed the exact dress and ornamentation worn by the different tribesmen and halfbloods; the kind of trade goods bartered to the Indians; the ways in which dogs were used; the methods of hunting and traveling in the area at different times of the year; the household arrangements within the tipis; the customs, dress, and equipment of the traders and settlers; and the physical look of the Colony itself at various times during the period that the Rindisbacher family lived there.

Peter apparently made many of his first sketches with pencil and pen and then copied them, again and again, in watercolor, usually making certain changes or adding new details in each copy. After his death, it was said by someone who had known him that he had had an aversion to oil, calling oil painting "smearing," possibly because of the crudeness of

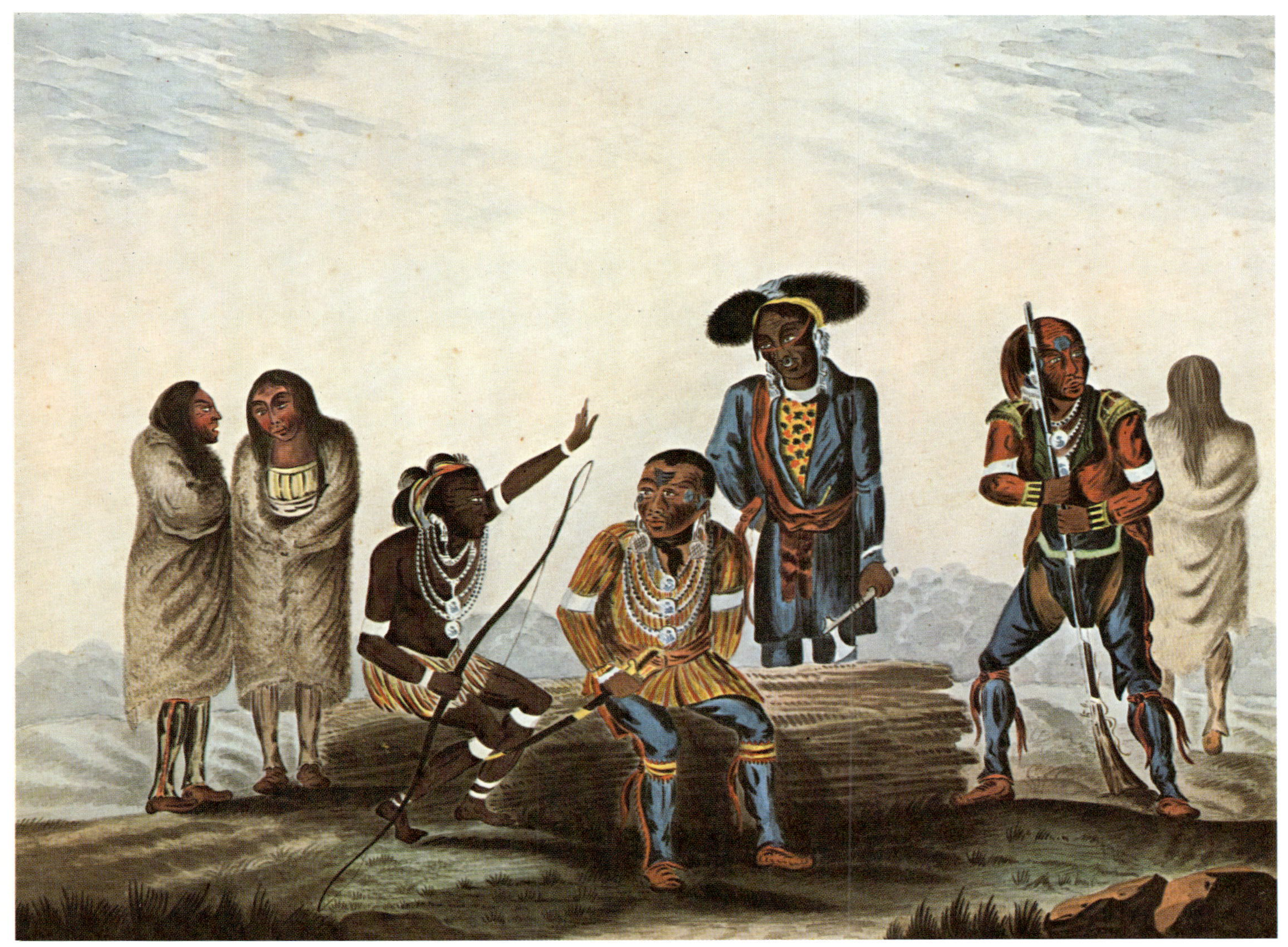

XIX. *Deputation of Indians from the Mississippi Tribes to the Governor General of British North America, Sir George Prevost, Bart., Lieut. General, in 1814.*
Watercolor, 15 x 18¾ inches, ca. 1822/1823.
Courtesy of the Missouri Historical Society, St. Louis.

pigments that had eventually become available to him. But at Red River he could not get the materials for oil painting, and was limited to the use of watercolors, which he employed not only for his new subjects but for the many copies and new versions of his earlier pen and pencil drawings.[34]

As he continued to paint, his work gained steadily in maturity, losing a certain youthful naïveté that had marked some of his first drawings, particularly of animals and native peoples. His landscapes and compositions of inanimate subjects and general scenes had always reflected the sureness and strength of an expert draftsman, but now he began to breathe a marvelous realism of expression and action into his living subjects. His father may have given him instruction in anatomy, for some of his best pictures portray men and animals in violent motion. Most characteristic of his later paintings, perhaps, are the modeled, three-dimensional effects of his figures; had they been done in recent times, it might be thought that the artist had employed an airbrush in his work.

"We see Indians engaged in murderous combat in hordes, swinging skull crushing clubs or the terrible tomahawk," wrote one of his early admiring critics.[35] "We see them individually or on horse in battle, piercing each other's naked bodies with arrows and spears. Then imitating war in games and dances, brandishing lethal weapons to the rhythms of drumbeat and battle songs. . . . His bison or so called buffalo hunts instruct us in the very temper of that animal. There we see them grazing peacefully in whole herds. Here, tracked and pursued by hunters, they flee with powerful leaps through the high grass of the prairies and bushes or through deep snow. Now a bull is wounded and charges his enemy in wild rage. Here again, a bison is attacked by dogs and in battle with them. And in all these representations, every movement of man and beast is captured artfully, and each muscle seems to be straining and all is agreeably contracted with a firm, but untutored sense of perspective . . . attitudes are shown naturally and with strength. . . . His portraits are full of expression — softly modeled from deep shadow to brightest light, true to nature and with eloquent resemblances. Each hair on a bison or deer or otter or dog appears to be individually shaded and seems to glow. The feathers of birds are so cleverly done that one imagines one sees a shimmer of color. Everything cheers the spirit and pleases the eye. The melting of soaring clouds in the landscapes, the transparent air and distances, the swelling of the earth, the charm of plant life, the desolateness of snow — all is pure depiction of nature whom he chose for his one and only teacher."

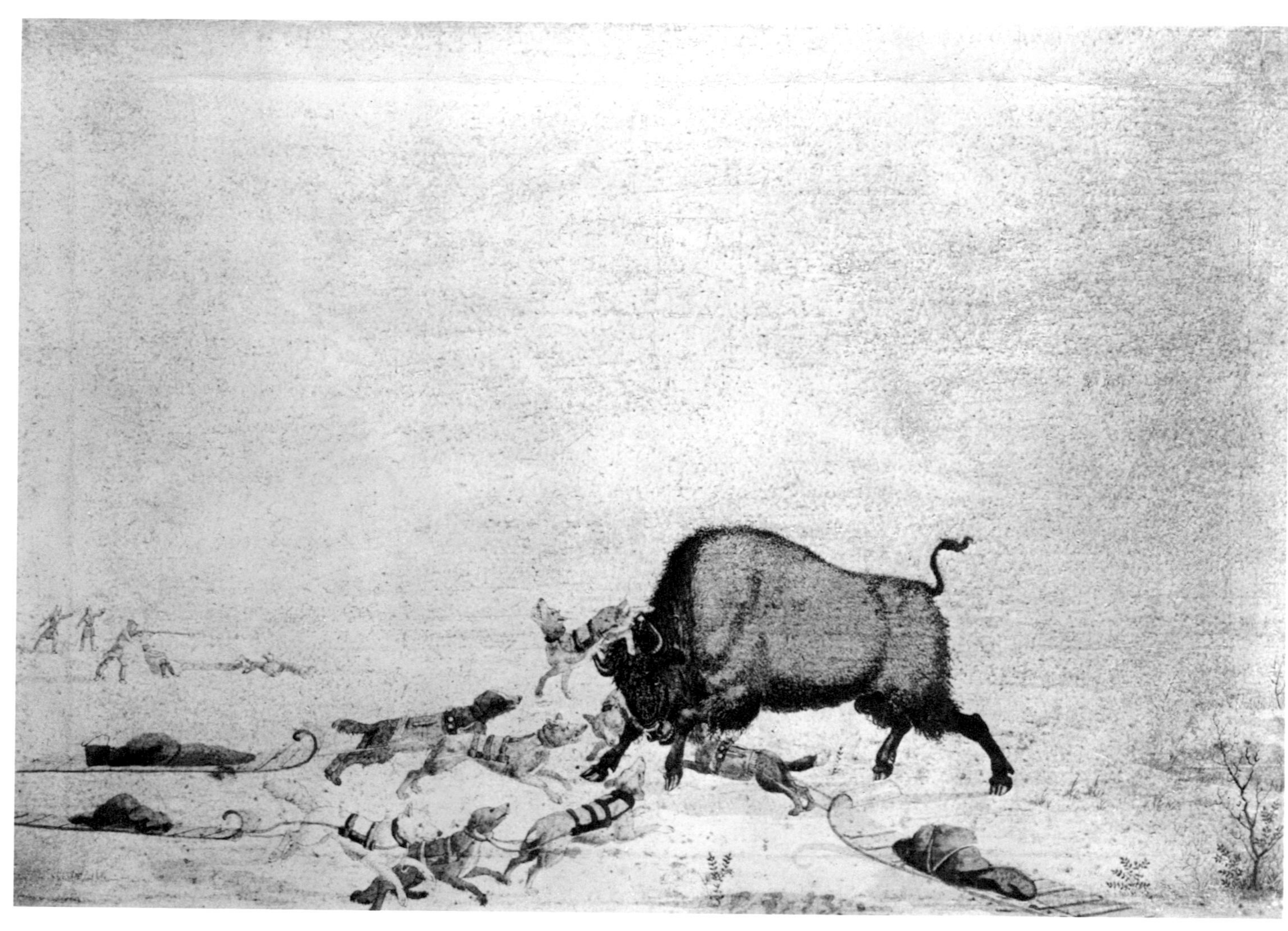

XX. *Sled Dogs Attacking a Bison Bull.*
Watercolor, 10½ x 15 inches, ca. 1823.
Courtesy of Hudson's Bay Company, Winnipeg.

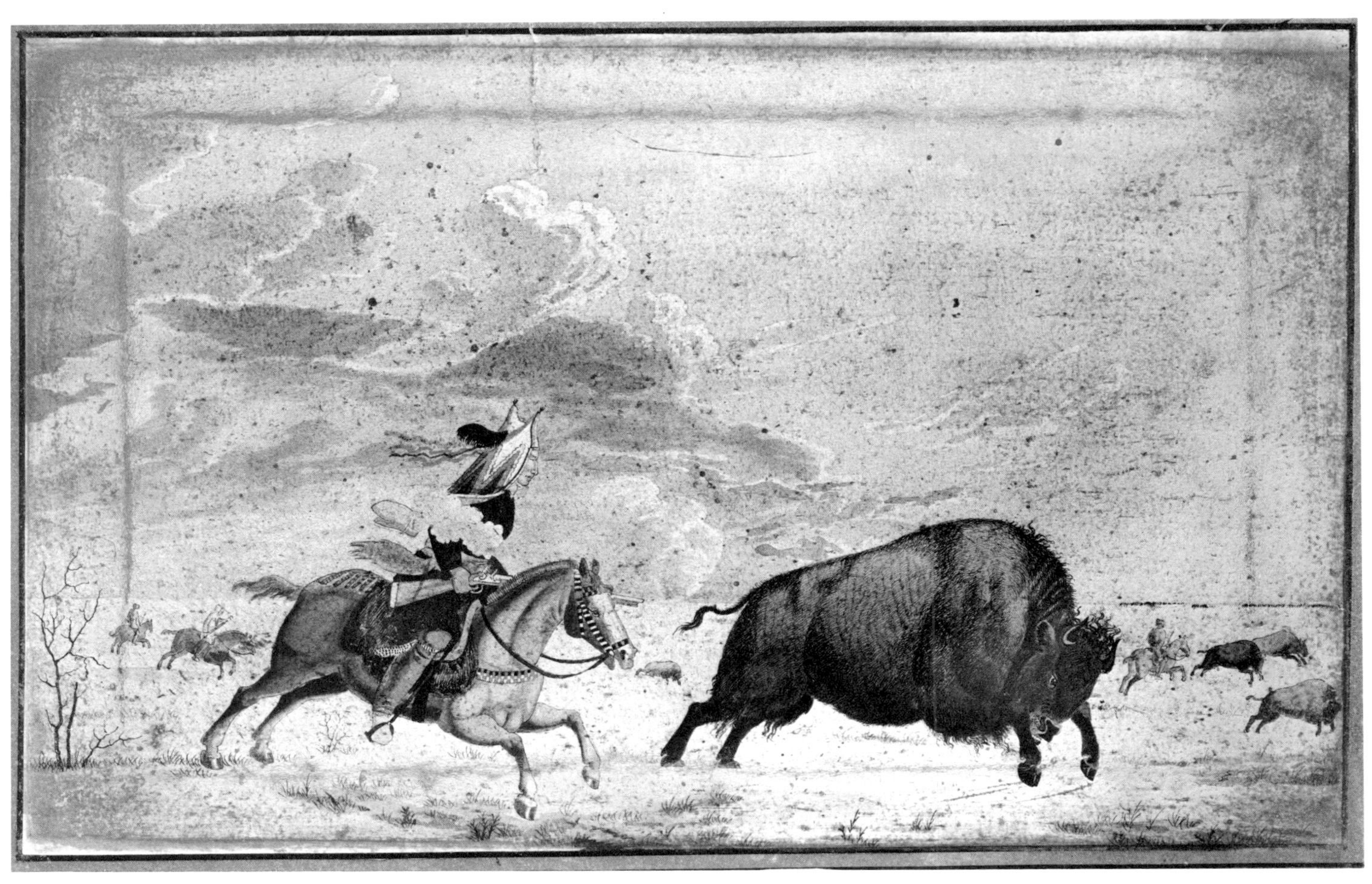

XXI. *Indian Hunter Killing a Bison.*
Watercolor, 7⅝ x 12 inches, ca. 1823.
Courtesy of Hudson's Bay Company, Winnipeg.

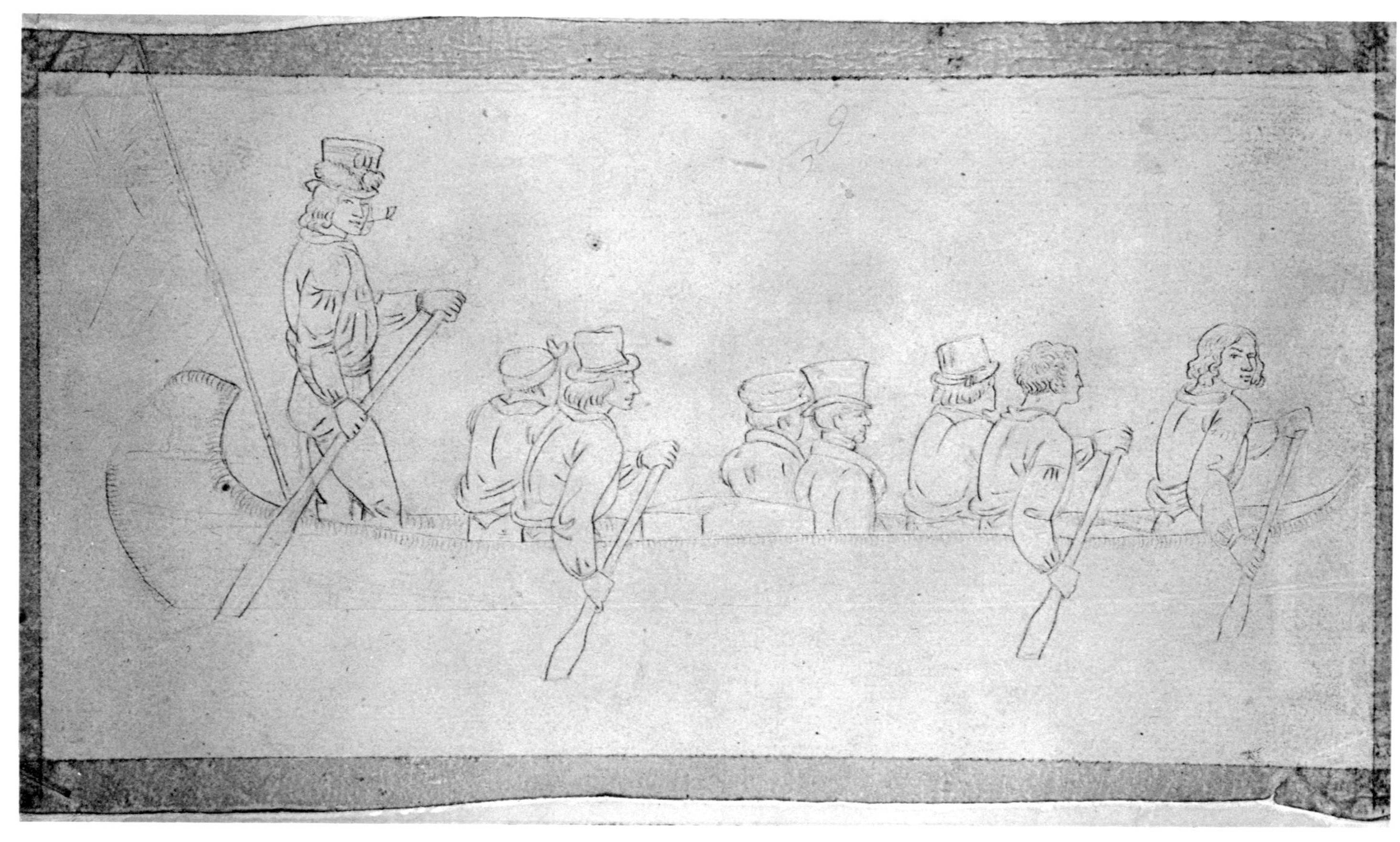

XXII. Men paddling canoe [Untitled].
Pencil study for the watercolor (right), 5½ x 9½ inches, ca. 1823.
Courtesy of Glenbow-Alberta Institute, Calgary.

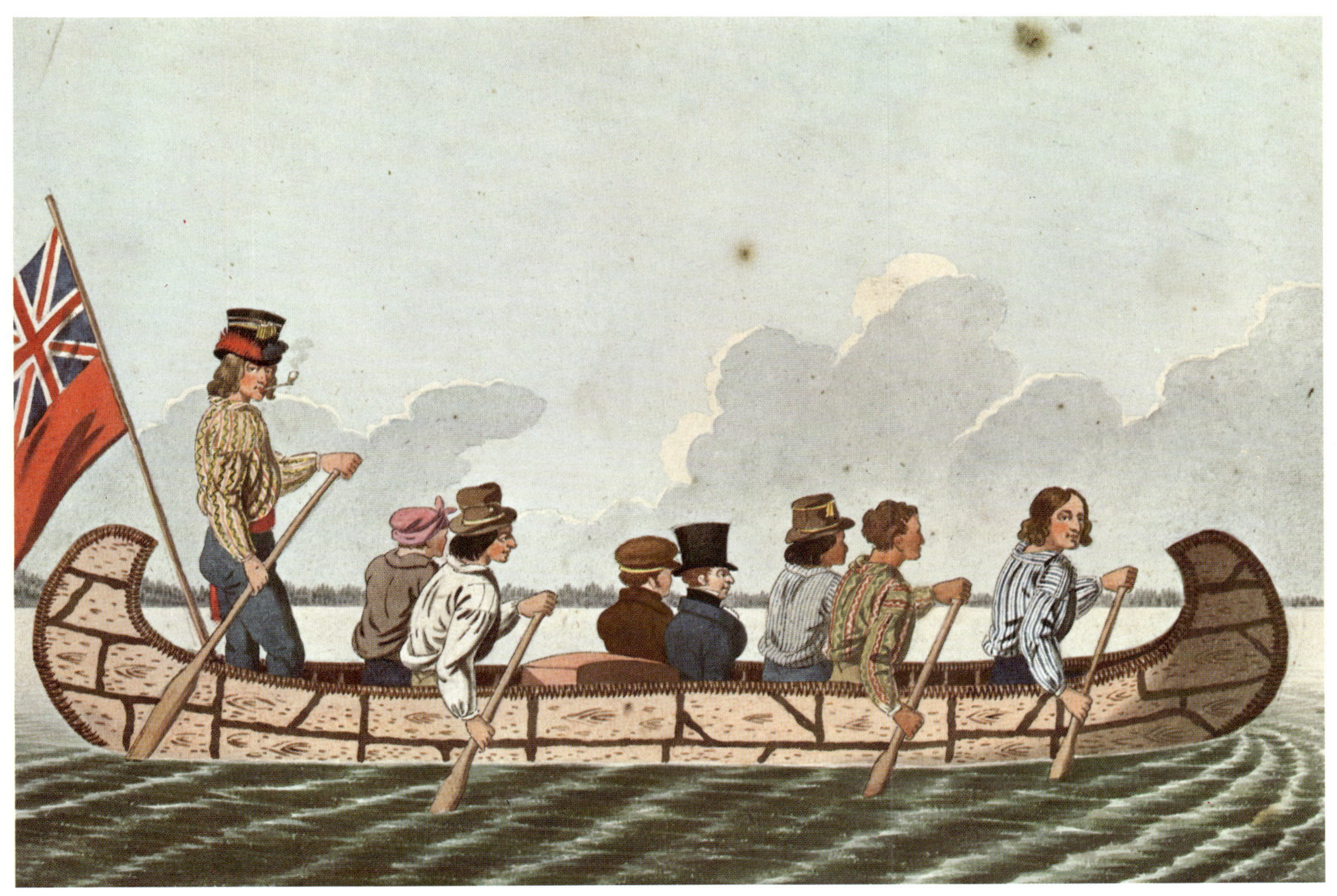

XXIII. *Two of the Companies Officers Travelling in a Canoe Made of Birchbark Manned by Canadians.*
Watercolor, 7¼ x 10⅜ inches, ca. 1823.
Courtesy of M. Knoedler and Co., Inc., New York.

Peter's drawings soon brought him a measure of celebrity in the Colony. The realism and accuracy with which he depicted the familiar scenes of the Indians and the Red River region gained the admiration of the settlers and fur traders who were his neighbors, and they began to ask "the boy artist," as they called him, for copies of his work. At first, he may have given away copies, including the set that the Reverend West took back to England with him in 1823. But eventually some of the Hudson's Bay Company officials who saw his work at Fort Garry commissioned copies, as well as original paintings, from him.

One of his first patrons was Captain Andrew Bulger, a veteran British officer of the War of 1812, who in 1822 succeeded Alexander Macdonell as Governor of the Red River Colony. Bulger took an interest in Peter's work and, becoming fond of the youth, gave him commissions for original paintings. Either then, or prior to Bulger's arrival, Peter was hired as a clerk at Fort Garry, but the job did not preclude his finding free time in which to draw. Bulger, in fact, is believed to have organized a special hunting party of Indians and halfbloods to take Peter out on the plains so the young artist could observe and paint the scenes of a buffalo hunt. It is possible that this was Peter's first exposure to some of the settings and action of the chase that he depicted in so many of his paintings.[36]

At the same time, some of the scenes of the Governor's life around Fort Garry that Bulger had Peter record became among the best known of Rindisbacher's Red River works — views of the Governor being paddled by Hudson's Bay employees in a light birchbark canoe; being pulled over the snow in a dog-drawn cariole; receiving Chippewa Indians from Minnesota's Red Lake district; conferring inside Fort Douglas with the same Indians; and driving his family in a horse-drawn cariole. During this period, also, Bulger commissioned Peter to make a curious adaptation of one of those paintings and turn it into a rendering of an historic event that the artist had not seen. From November, 1814, until the end of the War of 1812, Bulger had commanded Fort McKay at Prairie du Chien on the upper Mississippi River, and Bulger had Peter adapt his view of the reception of the Red Lake Chippewa Indians outside Fort Douglas to a scene of Bulger saying farewell to his Indian allies when he abandoned Fort McKay at the close of the War of 1812.[37] It was one of Rindisbacher's few attempts to portray an occurrence that he had not witnessed.

In 1823 Bulger left the Colony, apparently taking some of Rindisbacher's paintings with him. Two oil paintings, copies of the scenes of Bulger greeting the Red Lake Chippewas outside Fort Douglas and meeting with them inside the fort, were revealed among the possessions

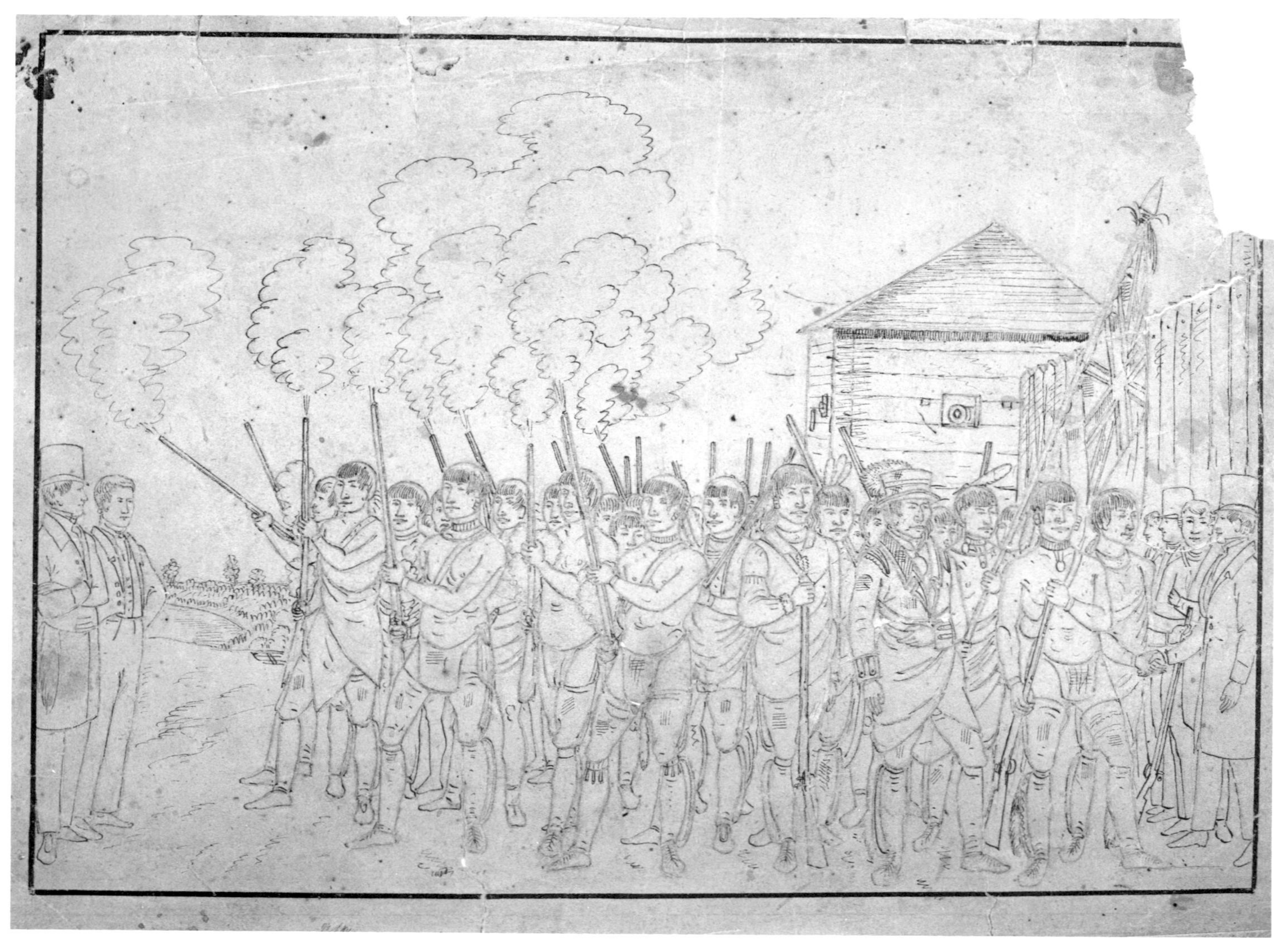

XXIV. The Red Lake Chief with some of his followers arriving at Red River and visiting the governor. [Untitled].
Pen and ink over pencil, 10¼ x 13½ inches, ca. 1823.
Courtesy of the Reverend and Mrs. Peter Dally, Vashon Island, Washington.

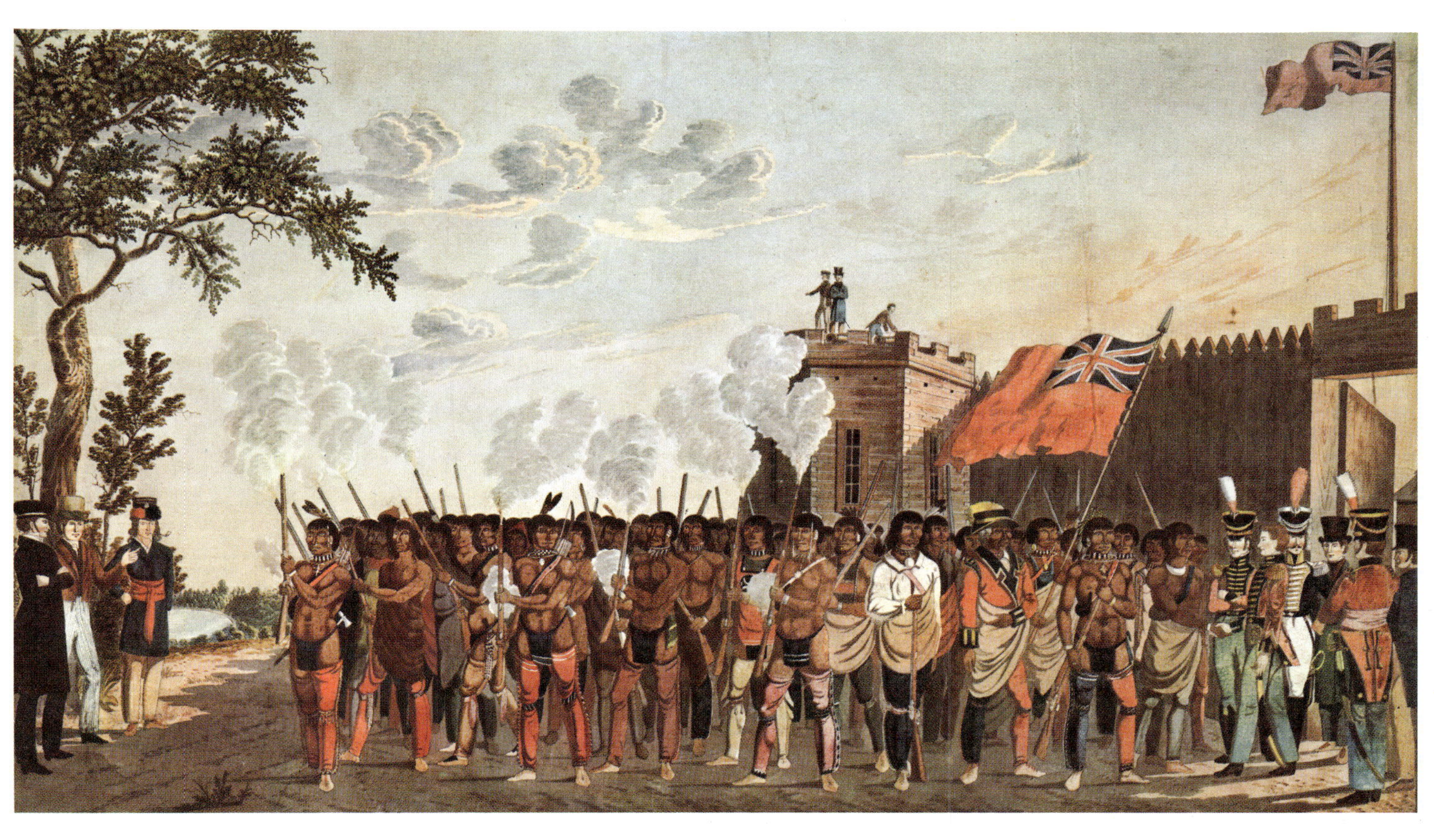

**XXV. Captain W. Andrew Bulger saying farewell to the chiefs and principal
Indian warriors at Fort MacKay, Prairie du Chien, Wisconsin, on 22 May 1815 [Untitled].**
Pen and watercolor, 14¼ x 23⅞ inches, ca. 1823.
Collection of Amon Carter Museum, Fort Worth.

of W. A. Bulger of Biggar, Saskatchewan, a descendant of the Governor, in 1945, but it is not known whether Rindisbacher or a later artist made the oil copies.[38] For a time, William Kempt, the sheriff at the Colony from 1822-24, also filled the role of acting Governor. Kempt acquired at least six of Peter's paintings, including a colorful buffalo-hunting scene in which the Indian or Métis hunter was shown wearing a double-peaked head covering, an article of dress unique to that area. These paintings, all done in Rindisbacher's usual style, in which he first made careful pencil and pen-and-ink outlines and then filled in the pictures with watercolors, were varnished over thickly by Kempt to protect them during his canoe trip from Red River to York Factory when he left the Colony for England. In 1934 one of Kempt's descendants gave them to the Hudson's Bay Company, and soon afterward they were sent to the company museum in Winnipeg for exhibition.

Late in 1823 Bulger's official successor, Robert Parker Pelly, arrived at the Colony as the new Governor. Pelly saw copies of the paintings that Peter had done for Bulger, and he ordered a set of six of them for himself. When he, too, returned to England in 1825, he commissioned an artist in that country, H. Jones, to make copies of Rindisbacher's paintings, but had him substitute Pelly for Bulger as the central figure in the scenes. He then had Jones's copies made into a set of six colored lithographs by W. Day of 59 Great Queen Street, London. The lithographs, issued as *Views in Hudson's Bay*,[39] are stilted and obviously less lifelike copies — with the substitution of Pelly's face and changes in other details — of Rindisbacher's scenes of the Governor of the Red River Colony meeting inside and outside Fort Douglas with the Red Lake Chippewas; traveling in a canoe in summer and in a dog-drawn cariole in winter; and driving his family in a horse-drawn cariole. The sixth subject is a copy of a Rindisbacher view of "A Souteaux [Chippewa] Indian, Traveling with his Family in Winter near Lake Winnepeg."

Pelly sent copies of the lithographs, or possibly the original Rindisbacher or Jones drawings, to the Governor and Committee of the Hudson's Bay Company in London, and on June 20, 1827, the Secretary of the Committee thanked him for "the drawings illustrative of the customs, &c of some of the tribes of Indians in the territory of the Company."[40] Sets of the lithographs, made up as books and selling for £ 1 each, were also sent to York Factory and Red River, where they were purchased by officials of the Hudson's Bay Company. They proved very popular, and in time became collectors' items. Bearing the signature of H. Jones, rather than of Rindisbacher, they played their role in contributing to the veil of obscurity that eventually settled over the name of the original artist, and it is only in comparatively recent years that it has been demonstrated that the lithographs, which now bring high prices at auction sales, were truly derived from Rindisbacher originals.

In Canada, correspondence now in the archives of the Champlain Society in Toronto reveals the extent of the interest in Peter's paintings among Hudson's Bay Company men. They not only bought the lithographs, but letters show that they were ordering watercolor originals and copies from the young artist. Much of their correspondence was directed to James Hargrave, the accountant at Fort Garry, who passed on their requests to Peter.[41]

On November 14, 1824, for instance, George Barnston of the Hudson's Bay Company wrote Hargrave from York Factory as follows:

> "Do not forget if you please my commission about the Drawings. The ones I should like to have in particular are — the Plain Indian on Horseback shooting at an enemy — the Group of Indians where the Scalp is introduced. Captain Bulger's Palaver — the death of the buffalo and two or three Buffaloes Pieces in which I think the lad excells — as also traveling in winter with an Indian Guide before the sled — Of all these I have seen several different copies, so that I conclude he keeps one copy to take another form as occasion may require."[42]

Barnston was, of course, correct in this surmise. Peter seems to have retained all or many of his original pen and pencil sketches, as well as certain watercolor copies, and he apparently kept them in his possession until his death, when his family acquired them. From the originals Peter continued to make copies throughout his life, and some of the best and most mature watercolors he ever made were copies that he did only in the last years of his life from the same originals to which Barnston referred. Barnston was also interested in new ideas for subjects, and he went on to Hargrave:

> "A Subject at which I have not as yet seen any attempt of his, and which I should like much to have is — Assiniboines stealing Horses — perhaps you might propose it to him. If care were taken upon it, I would willingly double the usual price — You may go to the length of £6 — in making purchases of this kind for me, but I beg you may be as liberal if not more so, than what others have been — I have a small drawing Box with a few Cakes of Paint, which is at the Young mans service if he is in want of anything of the Kind, and which can be easily forwarded to him by the Boats in Summer. By offering it as coming from yourself he may make less difficulty in accepting of it than if it were coming from a stranger."[43]

It is not known if Peter obliged by painting the scene of Assiniboines stealing horses, but in February and April, 1826, Barnston wrote to

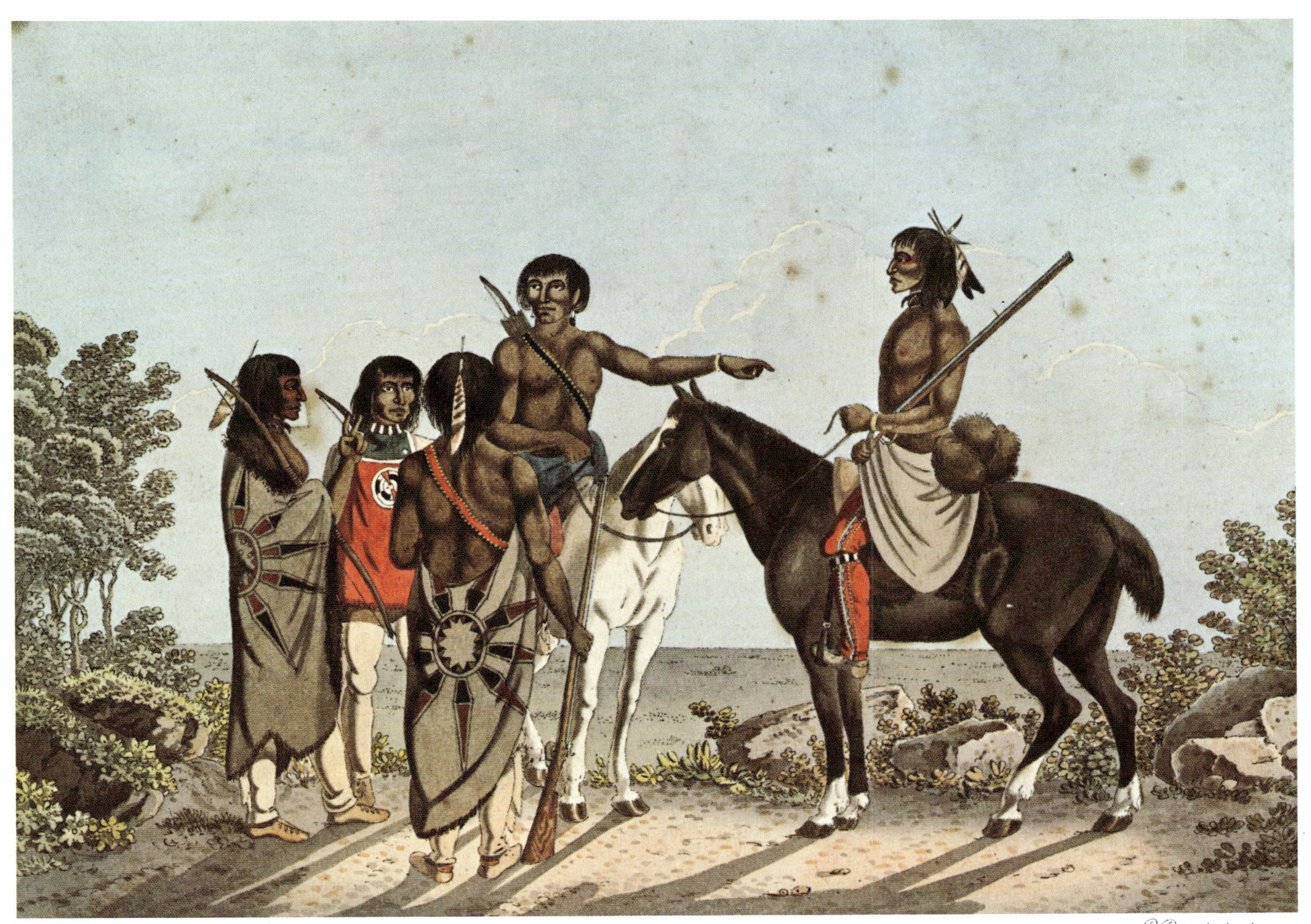

XXVI. *A Party of Indians—Asseneboines.*
Watercolor, 7⅞ x 9⅞ inches, ca. 1820/1825.
Courtesy of M. Knoedler & Co., Inc., New York.

Hargrave again about additional Rindisbacher paintings, offering to buy as many works as he could get for £15. Barnston must have accumulated many Rindisbacher paintings, which he hung in his homes, first in western Canada and then in Montreal. After his death in 1883, the works remained in his family. They are known to have included a set of the H. Jones lithographs, as well as watercolor copies of some of the original sketches that Peter had made during his trip from York Factory to Red River in 1821, including views of York Factory, Norway House, "Rockfort" and "Camp on Shores Lake Winnipeg." In 1942 all of them were lost when a fire destroyed the home of Barnston's granddaughter.

In September, 1826, Hargrave also wrote to Henry Boulton, who had been at York Factory too, sending him some of Peter's paintings and telling him that he could have purchased more of them if it had not been for disastrous floods that had inundated the Red River Colony the previous spring. As a result of the floods, the Rindisbachers and other families had finally had enough, and "the young lad together with his father and the whole of the family," Hargrave explained to Boulton, "has left the River for the United States so that these which you received are the last by that young Artist which will be procured in this country."[44]

Still, interest in Peter's work continued to be reflected in Hargrave's correspondence. References in his letters show that another purchaser of Peter's drawings in 1826 was William Smith, Secretary of the Hudson's Bay Company in London, although it is not known whether he was buying the works for himself or the company. In addition, Hargrave's correspondence in the Champlain Society archives reveals that "Pelly's picture books," the set of lithographs based on Rindisbacher originals, continued to be bought avidly by Hudson's Bay Company officials long after Peter had left the Red River.[45]

As noted earlier, the first discontented colonists to abandon the Red River Colony and head southward had been the five families who had left the settlement soon after their arrival in 1821. In the spring of 1823, thirteen more Swiss families, including the Monniers, Simons, Chetlains, and Schirmers, decided to leave the Colony and migrate to Missouri, whose climate and opportunities the cattle drovers had described glowingly two years before. They hired about six of the big, two-wheeled, creaking Red River carts to carry their possessions and, guided by Métis, made their way up the Red River Valley to Lake Traverse and the head of the St. Peter's (Minnesota) River.

On the United States side of the border their route lay through the hunting grounds of the Sisseton Sioux Indians. It was a bad year for the whites to be entering their country. The Sioux were being harried by their Sauk and Fox enemies and, in an angry mood, the Sisseton war bands hung on the settlers' flanks and threatened them with violence. The armed colonists guarded their train carefully, and at night even elderly women stood watch. Attacks were warded off by giving the Indians presents of food, ammunition and various trinkets, but on occasion provisions and articles of campware, including cooking utensils, were stolen by individual Indians. Eventually, the Swiss got through the most dangerous territory and at Lake Traverse gave up the carts, which were returned to Red River by their owners, and built dugouts from cottonwood trees. They floated down the St. Peter's in the dugouts, and in September safely reached Fort St. Anthony, where they were warmly welcomed by the families who had preceded them in 1821 and by the troops of the American garrison.[46]

Another group, composed of the families of David Tully and Robert Campbell, Scottish settlers who had come to Red River in 1819 under a three-year contract with Lord Selkirk to develop a farm at the Colony, was not so fortunate. Grasshoppers, near-starvation, and a string of miseries at the Colony had decided them to depart for the United States as soon as their contract ended, and in the spring of 1823 they, too, set off up the Red River with horses and Red River carts.[47] At Pembina, their guide's horses ran away. While Campbell and the guide went out on the plains to look for the horses, the Tullys, accompanied by two young halfblood guides, decided to journey on to the Grand Forks on the Red River, where they heard there was a large camp of buffalo-hunting Métis. There, they would secure enough meat for the remainder of the journey and wait for the Campbells to join them.

The Tully group had nearly reached the Grand Forks when they ran into trouble. They had camped late in the afternoon near the bank of the frozen river when a war band of Sissetons appeared. Tully ordered everyone to run for the river and cross on the ice to the opposite shore. The sudden movements induced the Indians to spur forward. As they came up on him, Tully fired at them, killing one of the Indians. The halfbloods got away, but the Sissetons made short work of the others. Pulling his two small sons, John and Andrew, with him, Tully tried to scramble across the ice, but fell into the water. As he clambered out again, he was shot by an angry Indian on the bank and disappeared under the ice for good. The two boys were pulled back off the ice by the Indians. Mrs. Tully was killed by an Indian's arrow even before she got out of camp. Her infant daughter and the two frightened boys were taken away as captives by the Indians, who first ripped up the camp and scattered everything about. Soon afterward, the Indians tired of the little girl's crying and killed her. They kept the boys until they were ransomed, John soon after his capture and Andrew some months later. Both boys were delivered to Major Lawrence Taliaferro, the U. S. Indian agent in the area. At Fort Snelling, where they were taken, John died of scarlet fever. Andrew was sheltered by the family of Captain Nathan Clark, and was eventually sent to New Orleans and New York, where he was reared in an orphan asylum and trained as a coach trimmer and harness maker.[48]

The Tully murders, in time, became the subject of one of Peter Rindisbacher's best known paintings. After the Campbells learned of the fate of the Tullys, they abandoned their plans to continue south that year and returned from Pembina to Red River, where their story of what happened created great excitement among the colonists. Peter undoubtedly listened to the details as they had first been related by the surviving halfbloods, and, responding to the settlers' morbid interest in the event, may immediately have depicted a version of the tragedy to sell to someone at the Colony. There is no way of being sure of this, however, and his original sketch may not have been made until he himself reached Fort Snelling three years later and found that the Tully affair was still so interesting a subject there that he drew a picture of it for someone at the post. At any rate, although his view of the attack on the Tullys was entirely imaginative and was another of the few pictures he made of scenes that he had not witnessed, his details of the Tullys' camp and equipage and of the Indians themselves were lifelike and accurate, and the work as a whole, portraying the impact of violence and terror on the Minnesota frontier, is one of his more dramatic paintings.

Meanwhile, the Swiss families who had reached Fort St. Anthony in safety proceeded on down the Mississippi River in keelboats provided by Colonel Snelling.[49] Some of the colonists died from sickness en route, and several had to be left temporarily in the post hospital at Fort Armstrong near the Sauk and Fox villages in Illinois. But the rest reached St. Louis in November and were hospitably received by some of that city's French-speaking citizens. There, too, however, the weather, hot, humid and unhealthful in summer, did not satisfy them, and in time they made another move. Among the people they met in St. Louis was Colonel Henry Gratiot, a member of a leading Missouri family that had come originally from Lausanne, Switzerland. In 1825, a year and a half after the Red River families arrived in St. Louis, a rush developed suddenly to large lead mines in the Winnebago Indian country of northwestern Illinois. In mid-October of that year, Henry Gratiot and his

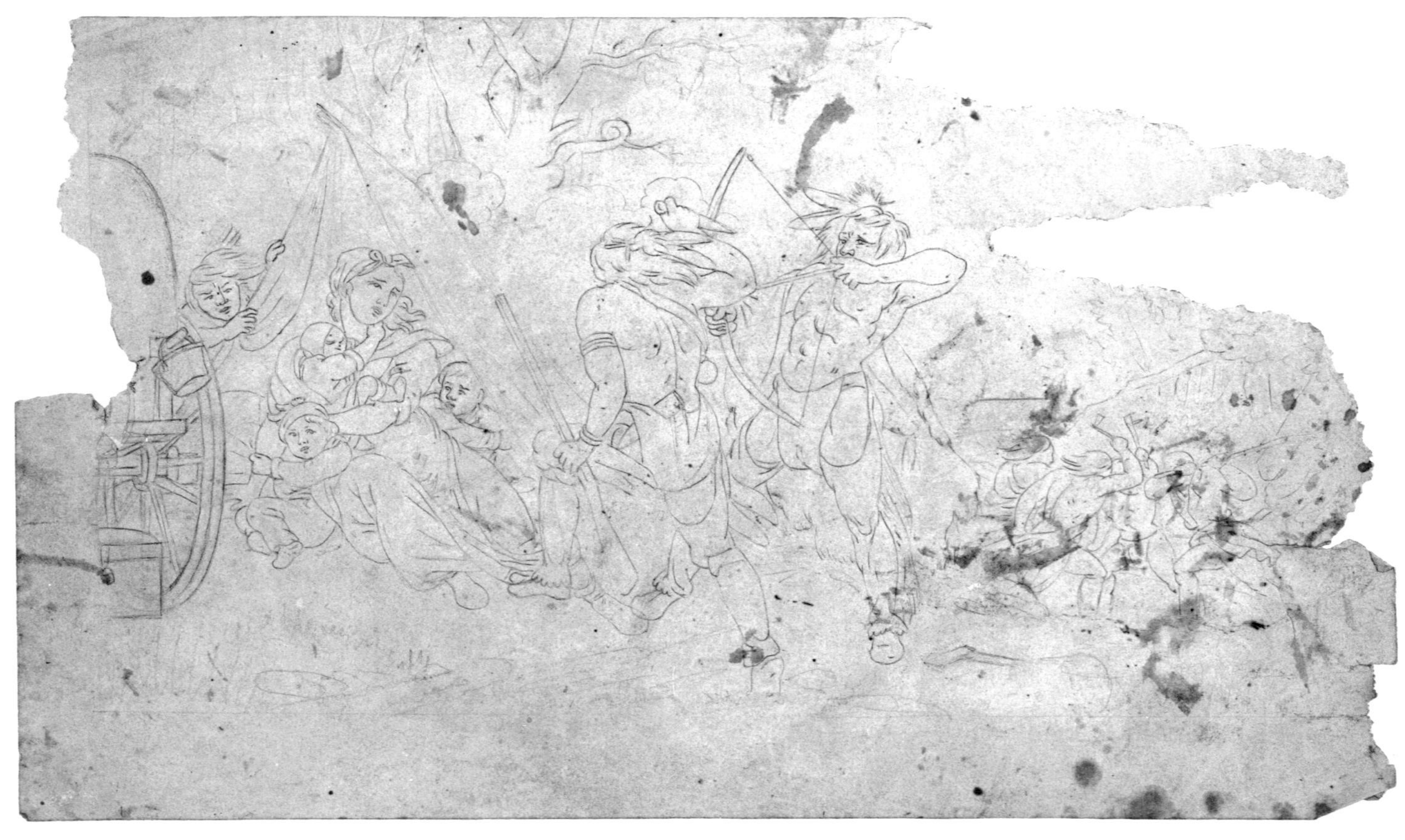

XXVII. The murder of David Tully and his family [Untitled].
Preliminary study for the watercolor (right).
Pencil, 7⁷⁄₁₆ x 12¼ inches, ca. 1823/1830.
Courtesy of the Reverend and Mrs. Peter Dally, Vashon Island, Washington.

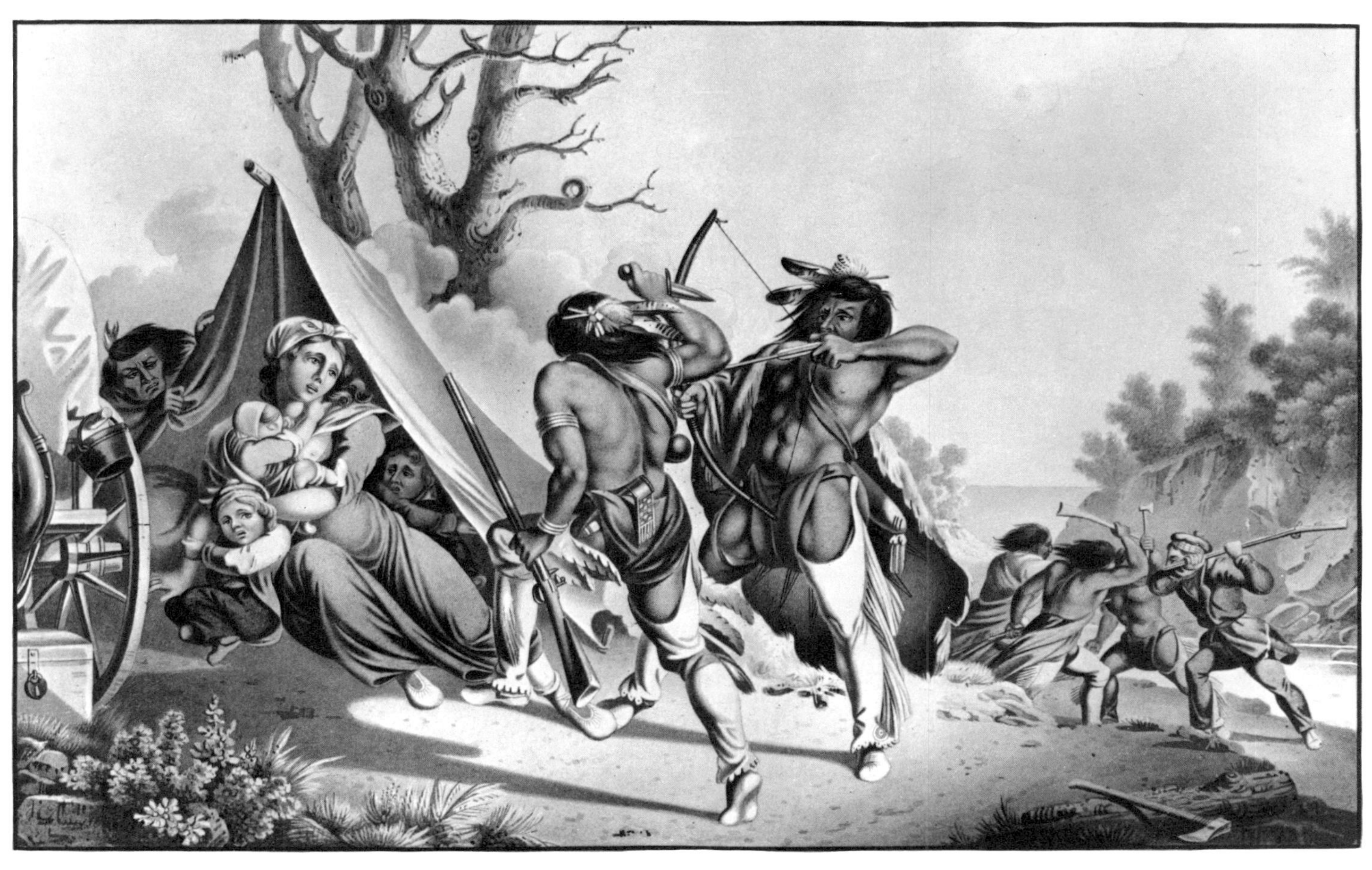

XXVIII. *The Murder of David Tally [Tully] and Family by the Sissetoons Sioux, a Sioux Tribe.*
Watercolor, 6½ x 11 inches, ca. 1823/1830.
Courtesy of West Point Museum, United States Military Academy, West Point, New York.

brother, John P. B. Gratiot, went with a two-horse wagon to the lead country to erect a smelter. They stayed in the frontier region all winter, building cabins and log furnaces for the smelter, and in the spring of 1826, Henry, now also appointed agent to the Winnebago Indians, went back to St. Louis to get his family.[50] Several of the Swiss colonists, hearing of the cooler and more healthful country around the lead mines, decided to go north with the Gratiots, and in April the Chetlains and a few other families departed on the steamboat *Mexico* up the Mississippi to the site of the present city of Galena, Illinois. A few months later, several other Swiss families in St. Louis followed them.

The region in which they settled centered around the Fever River, which today is still called the Fever in Wisconsin, but in Illinois was renamed the Galena in 1848.[51] During the summer of 1826 reports reached the miners that Winnebago Indians were taking out lead from even richer deposits on a prairie about 15 miles to the northeast. The Gratiots quickly made an agreement with the Indians to mine that area, and moved to the new district, which became known as Gratiot's Survey and then Gratiot's Grove. A number of Swiss colonists followed the Gratiots to that area and erected cabins for themselves.

"About this time," wrote Mrs. Adéle P. Gratiot, the wife of John P. B., in reminiscences which she recorded many years later, "came down from Fort Snelling [the renamed Fort St. Anthony], a number of Swiss families who had migrated to Lord Selkirk's settlement on the North Red River." Mrs. Gratiot was now referring to still another wave of emigrants from the Red River Colony, a new one in 1826 that finally included young Peter Rindisbacher and his family. "After suffering for several years from starvation, and from the several overflows of the river, destroying their crops, and almost destruction from the half breeds and fierce tribes surrounding," Mrs. Gratiot wrote, "they at last made up their minds to leave in a body. They were industrious, honest people, and a great acquisition to a new country. Henry Gratiot and my husband secured the services of several families, among whom was Peter Rendesbacher [*sic*], afterwards so celebrated for his pictures of Indians and other works of art."[52]

The Rindisbachers, who had clung so long to their home on Red River, had finally been driven out by one of the worst disasters the region has ever experienced. During the winter of 1825-26 the area had been blanketed by unusually heavy snowstorms. Then, in May, 1826, there was a sudden thaw which, failing to melt the ice in the rivers, covered the prairies with sheets of water. The rising floods were made worse by storms of driving rain, accompanied by lightning, thunder and heavy

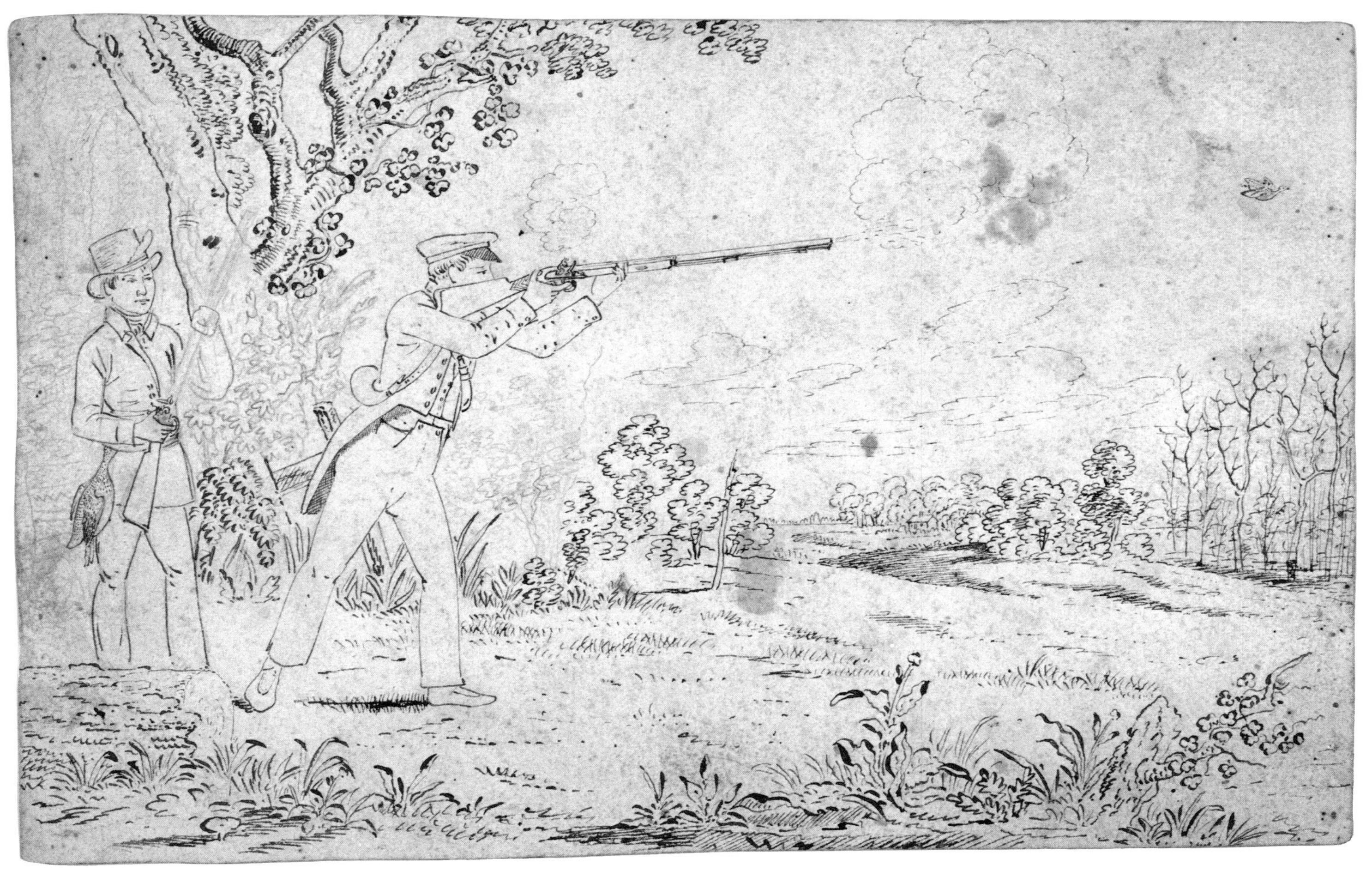

XXIX. Two young men hunting [Untitled].
It is likely that the artist has pictured himself here in the act of shooting quail.
Pen and ink over pencil, 7 x 10¾ inches, ca. 1823.
Courtesy of Mrs. Frances Rindesbacher Eustice, Cleveland Heights, Ohio.

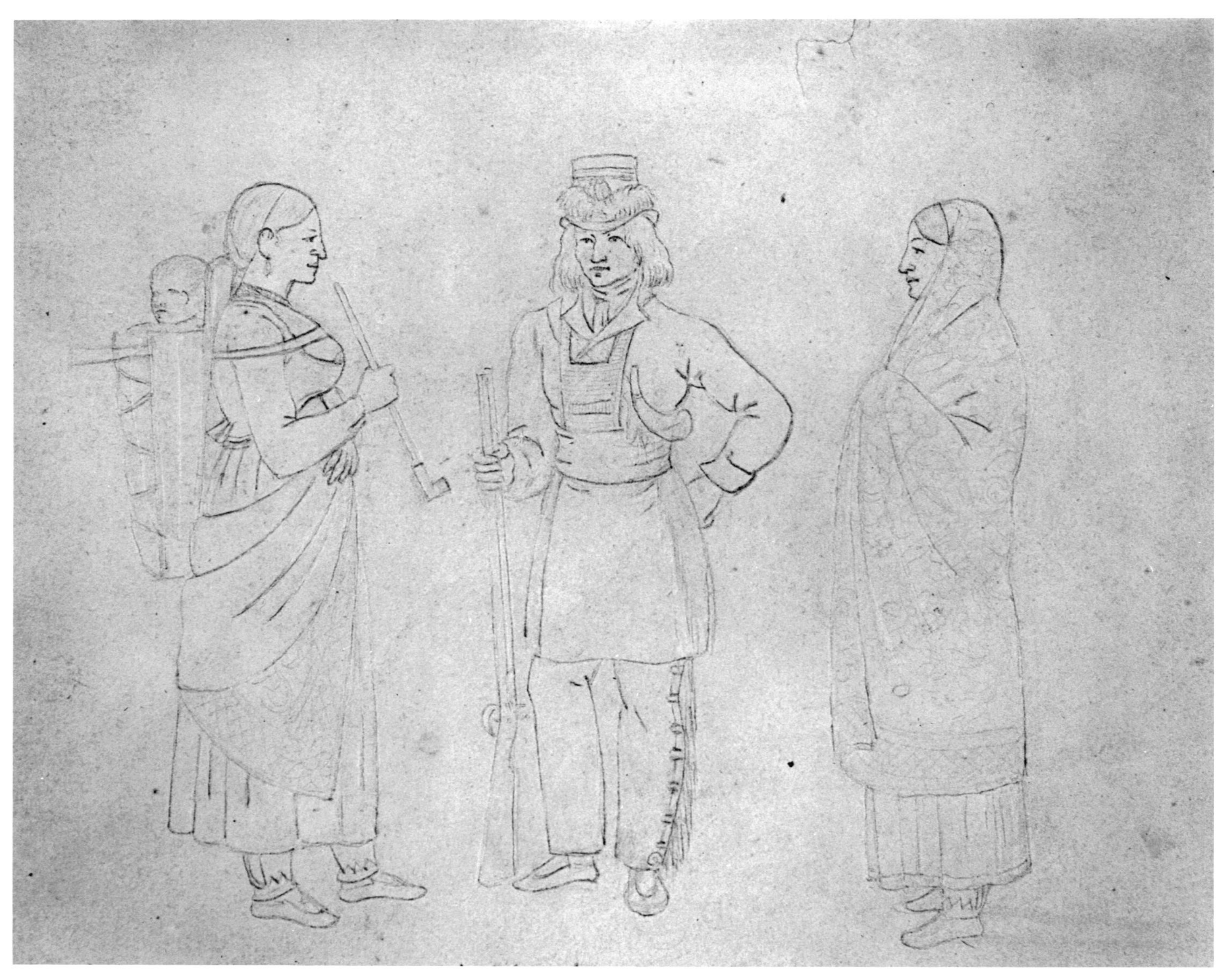

XXX. Man with two women [Untitled].
Pencil, 6½ x 7½ inches, ca. 1825/1826.
Courtesy of Glenbow-Alberta Institute, Calgary, Alberta.

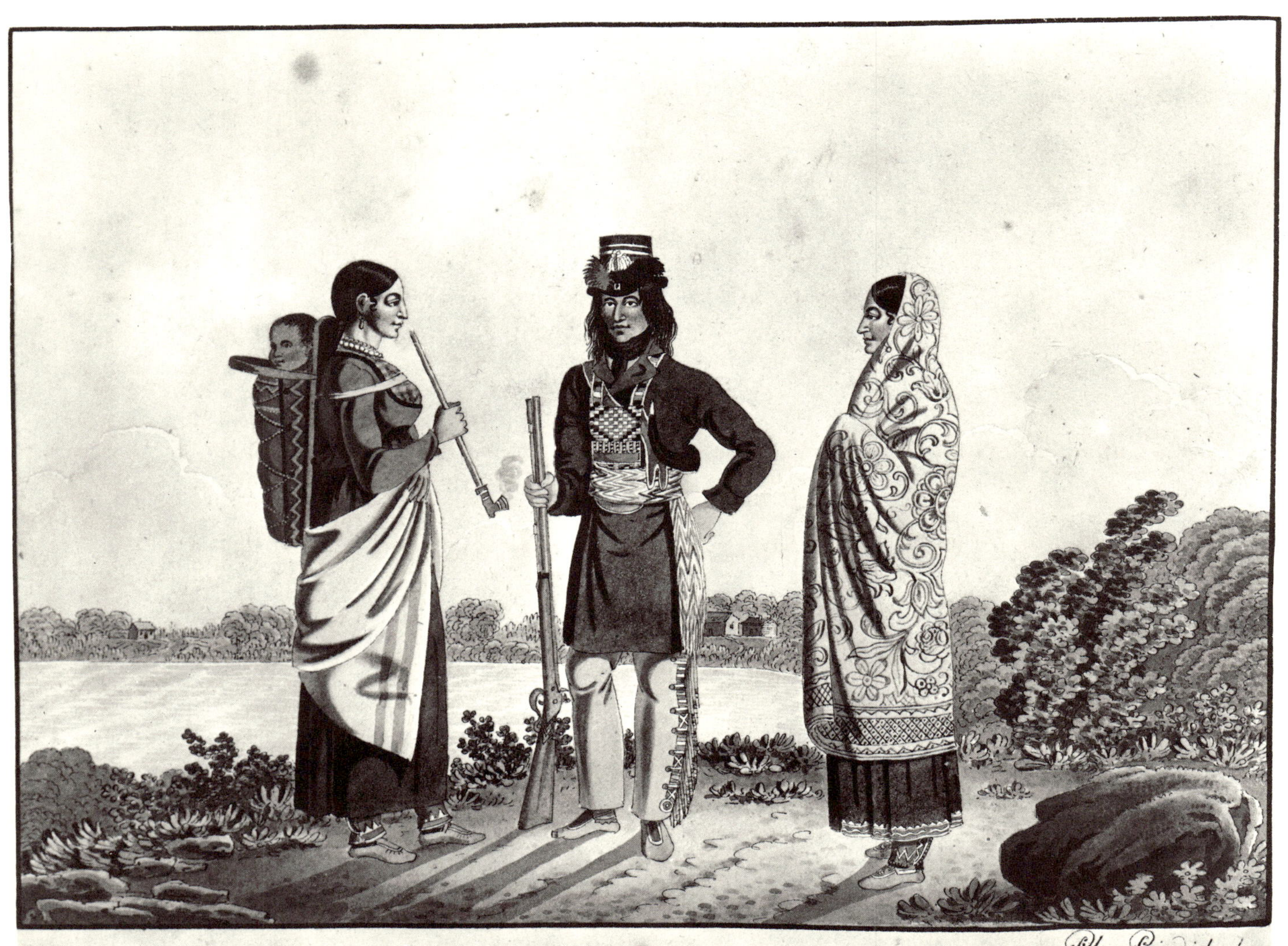

XXXI. *A Halfcast and His Two Wives.*
Watercolor, 7 x 9 inches, ca. 1825/1826.
Courtesy of M. Knoedler and Co., Inc., New York.

winds. The waters rose to record levels, forcing the colonists to flee to higher ground, and washing away their homes and fields. In a few days all their labor of years had vanished. When the storms finally ended and the waters began to subside, fewer than ten homes had been spared by the flood. All the others were in ruins or had disappeared.[53] The settlers surveyed the damage and began courageously to rebuild and replant. Then a new misfortune struck them; in the course of a single night grubworms destroyed their new fields of barley and potatoes. The Rindisbachers and many others had at last suffered enough. In July they decided to leave for the United States. Selling their cattle and farm equipment and hiring carts, 23 families, apparently under the leadership of Peter's father, their senior member, departed from the Colony on July 11.[54] The Governor supplied them with provisions at no cost and gave them an interpeter and an armed escort of forty-five men for their journey to the south.[55]

Like those who had left the Colony in previous years, they traveled to the St. Peter's River, making the crossing of the Sioux country without trouble, and arrived safely at Fort St. Anthony, which had now been renamed Fort Snelling. There the colonists learned about the settlements that their predecessors had made with the Gratiots in the Fever River country, and they decided to join them. A small steamboat took them down the Mississippi from Fort Snelling to the mouth of the Fever River, which they reached in November. Some of the families traveled on to Gratiot's Grove, but the Rindisbachers wintered at the smelter, working for the Gratiots, and in the spring moved to the Grove where they built a home and prepared to farm.[56]

IV. YEARS AT GRATIOT'S GROVE

Peter, it seems clear, had brought with him from Red River a portfolio of originals or copies of all his drawings, and at Fort Snelling and Fort Crawford, another American army post which the travelers passed on the Mississippi River near Prairie du Chien, he had possibly made sales of his work to members of the garrison.[57] At those posts, it may be speculated, soldiers had examined his paintings of Indian scenes and wildlife, regarding them as realistic portrayals of the frontier on which they were serving, and it is not unlikely that more than one of them paid him to make copies, much as a person today might purchase postcards or prints from a photographer, either to send home to family or friends, or to retain as personal mementos. Furthermore, as will be related shortly, a number of army officers serving in the Mississippi Valley were soon to be instrumental in gaining a wider audience in the United States for Peter's work, and it may well be that the artist first met and attracted the interest and patronage of one or more of them during this trip from Red River to the Gratiot settlement.

At any rate, in his new home, close to the western end of the present boundary between Illinois and Wisconsin, and in country frequented by Winnebago and Sauk and Fox Indians, Peter found new subjects to paint.[58] At the same time, he also seems to have done a number of miniature portraits, some on ivory, of friends and neighbors. His small paintings of Indians, animals and birds continued to arouse curiosity and admiration. But there was also apparently a ready market among the settlers for his realistic, delicately-wrought portraits of members of their families. Within a few years, the artist was celebrated in the area both for his miniature likenesses and for his Indian and wildlife scenes.[59]

The Winnebago country was not without its alarms and troubles. In 1827 the Indians' resentment over the whites' rapid overrunning of their lands increased in intensity, and in July violence broke out. A number of whites were killed by a group of angry Winnebagos, and work ceased abruptly at the mines as the settlers hastily built blockhouses and raised picket defenses around their homes. In response to their appeals for assistance, nearly 700 troops of the First and Third Infantry Regiments under General Henry Atkinson were rushed up the Mississippi in three steamboats from Jefferson Barracks near St. Louis. While the soldiers, accompanied by mounted civilians from the Fever River district, combed the countryside, searching for the Indians who had attacked the settlers, some one hundred whites, mostly women and children, took one of the steamboats back to St. Louis.[60] We have no information concerning the activities of Peter, or members of his family, while these troubles swirled about them, but the excitement was soon over. The Indians surrendered several of their people, identifying them as those who had killed the whites, and by the end of September Atkinson and his troops were back in St. Louis. But the cause of the conflict remained, and the federal government decided to send commissioners to a formal treaty meeting with the affronted Indians and purchase from them the lands that the miners and settlers were overrunning.

The commission, appointed by President Andrew Jackson in May, 1829, included General John McNeil, whose First U.S. Infantry had replaced Snelling and the Fifth Infantry on the upper Mississippi River after the Winnebago excitement; Pierre Menard, a former fur trader, Kaskaskia merchant, and Lieutenant Governor of Illinois; and Caleb Atwater, a fifty year-old lawyer of Circleville, Ohio.[61] Atwater, who had long had an amateur's interest in the American Indians, traveled to St. Louis and then to Prairie du Chien, on the Mississippi River above the Fever River, where the treaty meeting was to take place. Somewhere along the way, he met Peter Rindisbacher and admired his paintings of Indians.

The meeting might have occurred in St. Louis. In early June of that year Peter made a visit to that city, where he stayed at the home of a friend from Fever River, Sarah Beebe, the daughter of a prominent St. Louis citizen named Stephen Hempstead, Sr., and the widow of Elijah Beebe. Making note in his diary of Peter's arrival in the city on June 1, and reflecting the reputation which the artist already possessed, Hempstead referred to him as "a minintor painter from Fever river," and recorded three days later that "I have been Siting to have my miniure takeing" to send to another daughter at Fever River.[62] Peter may already have intended to settle permanently in St. Louis and make a living there by his painting, and it is possible that, during his stay at this time, he did other miniature portraits besides that of Mr. Hempstead. But in July he was far up the Mississippi River again, painting Indians at the treaty meeting at Prairie Du Chien.

When he left St. Louis is not known. But on June 30, one of Stephen Hempstead's sons, Charles, who had been at school in St. Louis, departed from that city on the steamer *Missouri* for Fever River, where he intended to practice law. Since Charles was also hired as Secretary of the Commission, bound for the Prairie du Chien treaty sessions, it may be guessed that Atwater was aboard the same steamboat, and that another passenger was Peter Rindisbacher, perhaps already enlisted by Atwater to paint scenes at Prairie du Chien.[63]

On July 29 the Commission signed a land cession treaty with the Chippewas, Ottawas and Potawatomies at Prairie du Chien, and on August 1 a treaty with the Winnebagos. The land ceded by the latter tribe included districts already overrun in the Fever River country, and 42 sections in that area were soon granted to various white families. Peter's presence at the Prairie du Chien meetings is reflected both by the work he did there and by Atwater's allusions to him. In a book titled *The Writings of Caleb Atwater,* published at Columbus, Ohio, in 1833, Atwater included an account of his participation at the treaty sessions and his ensuing trip to the nation's capital with the signed treaties, which he called *Remarks made on a Tour to Prairie Du Chien; thence to Washington City in 1829*. In that account, originally written in 1831, he noted that he had taken East with him some paintings which he had had made at Prairie du Chien. They included "as correct likeness as I ever saw drawn" of various Sauk and Fox Indians, including the Sauk leader, Keokuk, and a halfblood Fox chief named Morgan, as well as a portrait of Isaac Winnesheek, the son of a Winnebago chief at Prairie Lacrosse. A suggestion that he had not thought of having the paintings made until after he had been at the treaty meetings is contained in a further note that his gratefulness for the Indians' cooperation at the meetings had been his "motive for being at the expense of these beautiful paintings" which, he added, had gone on to London "a year since," possibly meaning 1830.[64]

Twenty-one years after the publication of that book, Atwater provided further information both about those paintings and about the artist at Prairie du Chien. On July 24, 1854, in response to an invitation from Lyman C. Draper of the Wisconsin Historical Society to join that organization and contribute to its collection, Atwater, then 76 years old, sent Draper a copy of his *Tour to Prairie Du Chien* and "4 drawings of my favorites, natives of your region of country," apparently four paintings made by Rindisbacher at Prairie du Chien in 1829. They included the likeness of Isaac Winnesheek, tinted sketches of a prairie wolf and a waterfowl, called "Pattashgas of the Wisconsin," and, possibly, a drawing of a muskrat — though the latter has since been lost.[65] In his letter to Draper, Atwater wrote: "Winnesheek was my pet, and so was the Prairie Wolf. The latter I carried with me, as far as Edwardsville, where I left him, as I feared that the traveling any further with me, would kill him. My likenesses of Indians are in the Patent Office, at Washington City. I paid a painter one hundred and thirty dollars for his services, and I paid one hundred dollars for carriage of minerals, etc."[66]

On August 13, 1854, Atwater again wrote to Draper, discussing this time a painting to which he had referred in his *Tour to Prairie du Chien* when he had written of Sauk and Fox Indians, including Keokuk and Morgan, shown with "as correct likenesses as I ever saw drawn." It was a group scene in which seventeen Sauk and Foxes were pictured in a war dance. In 1837, eight years after Atwater had brought that painting back with him from Prairie du Chien, and three years after Peter had died, it had appeared, in a color lithograph attributed to "Rindisbacher," as the frontispiece for the first volume of the folio edition of *The Indian Tribes of North America, with Biographical Sketches and Anecdotes of the Principal Chiefs*, a three-volume collection of large plates of Indian paintings, published in Philadelphia by Edward C. Biddle for Thomas L. McKenney and James Hall. The picture had gained wide popularity and, without again being attributed to Rindisbacher, had been reproduced and copied a number of times after its first appearance. Now, in 1854, Atwater explained to Draper:

"The likenesses of 13 Indians [plus four seated drummers], Sauks & Foxes, in water colors, were given to Col. Childs [who in 1829 had established the lithographing firm of Pendleton, Kearney & Childs] of Philada who promised me to engrave the Picture & send me 25 copies of the print. It represented 13 of the Sauks & Foxes, in a war dance. Keokuk Morgan & others were drawn to the life, by my Swiss artist, Rhindesberger. Col. Childs carried the picture to England, where he published it, accompanied by a biographical sketch of each Indian written by me. On the Colonel's return, he sent only one copy which fell into the hands of James Hall of Cincinnati, who in co. with some engraver in Philada

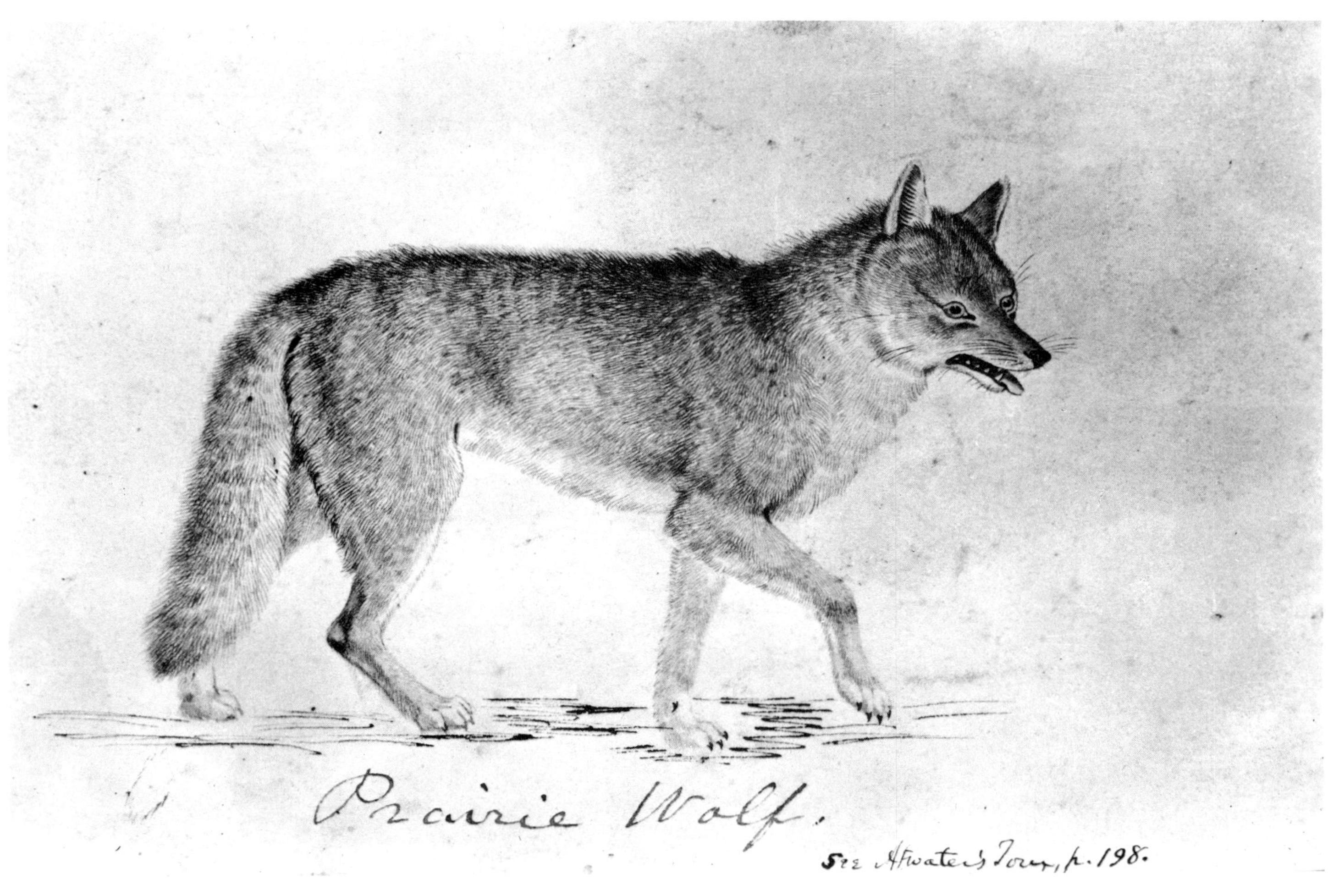

XXXII. *Prairie Wolf.*
Watercolor brushdrawing, 5¼ x 7¼ inches, ca. 1829.
Courtesy of the State Historical Society of Wisconsin, Madison.

published it in nos. of a magazine. The original picture and the engravings are in London and not in America."[67]

The plate of the "Sauk and Fox War Dance," published by McKenney and Hall, shows twelve Indians dancing vigorously around a central figure, while four seated Indians, at the left, drum and sing. As usual, Rindisbacher portrayed the clothing and the various weapons brandished by the Indians with exacting detail and fidelity. The plate carried an explanation by Caleb Atwater of the figures in the painting, but made no mention of the artist. In the text which McKenney and Hall furnished, however, the following, for which Atwater was undoubtedly the source, appeared:

> The picture which we have selected as a frontispiece for the first number of our series, is an accurate representation of one of the War Dances of the Winnebagoes,[68] drawn by Rhinedesbacher, a young Swiss artist, who resided for some years on the frontier, and attained a happy facility in sketching both the Indians and the wild animals of that region. This drawing is considered as one of his best efforts, and is valuable not so much as a specimen of art, in which respect it is in some particulars defective, as on account of the correct impression which it conveys of the scene intended to be represented. It was drawn on the spot as the scene was actually exhibited. The actors are persons of some note, and the faces are faithful likenesses.[69]

In 1839, another lithograph of the same painting appeared as the frontispiece for the second volume of the work, *Travels in North America During the Years 1834, 1835, & 1836*, published in London by Charles Augustus Murray. The British author, however, seems to have relied on a copy from the McKenney and Hall version, for he gave acknowledgment to that work.[70] What happened to Rindisbacher's original painting, which Atwater said that Childs had taken to London, presumably in 1830, is not presently known. In 1870, Henry Tuckerman's *American Artist Life* noted that James C. McGuire of Washington, D. C. owned a picture described as "Rindisbacker — Indian War Dance, 17 full-length figures, Portraits."[71] It was listed in the McGuire collection sales catalogue in 1888 as a painting fifteen by eight inches,[72] but in 1933 Frederick Hodge, in notes to a new edition of the McKenney and Hall plates, stated that "the original oil-painting [of the "Sauk and Fox War Dance"] is owned by Mr. Fred B. M'Guire, director of the Corcoran Gallery of Art, Washington, D. C., who received it from the estate of his father, James C. M'Guire, a noted collector of pictures."[73] There the trail ends, for in 1949 John Francis McDermott reported that the McGuire family no longer possessed the painting.[74] If the McGuire painting was an oil, it may be questioned whether it was, indeed, the original, or even a version done by Rindisbacher. One version of the painting does exist, a watercolor in a collection of Rindisbacher paintings owned by the West Point Museum. But this version seems to have been a copy made by Peter at a later date when he was in St. Louis. Like the seventeen other Rindisbacher watercolors in the West Point collection, its acquisition by the Academy is a mystery. The Museum has owned the group since at least 1898, when a catalogue of the Ordnance Museum first made note of possessing the paintings, but one can only speculate, as will be noted later, on the identity of the donor.

The second volume of the original McKenney and Hall folio edition carried, as its frontispiece, a colored lithograph of another Rindisbacher painting. This one, "Buffalo Hunt," depicting a mounted Indian closing in on a buffalo with drawn bow and arrow, while other Indians move through the rest of the herd in the distance, may have come to McKenney and Hall from a source other than Caleb Atwater. It is a scene of the plains country, and could not have been made in the region of Prairie du Chien. Two watercolor versions by Rindisbacher are known to exist, one in the West Point collection and the second a larger (18 by 30 inches) painting that Peter presented to Benjamin West Tingley of Philadelphia when that gentleman was in St. Louis.[75] But both vary so greatly in detail from each other, as well as from the lithograph, that it is thought that neither one could be the original from which the McKenney and Hall plate was made.

Again, in their text of the second volume, McKenney and Hall called attention to the artist of "Buffalo Hunt," who was now dead:

> The animating scene [a buffalo hunt] which we have endeavoured to describe, will be better understood by an inspection of the beautiful drawing of Rhinedesbacker, a young Swiss artist of uncommon talent, who, lured by his love of the picturesque, wandered far to the West, and spent several years upon our frontier, employing his pencil on subjects connected with the Indian modes of life. His was the fate of genius. His labours were unknown and unrequited. Few who saw the exquisite touches of his pencil knew their merit. They knew them to be graphic, but valued slightly the mimic presentation of familiar realities. They might wonder at the skill which placed on canvas the war dance, or the buffalo hunt, but they could not prize as they deserved, the copies of exciting scenes which they had familiarly witnessed. Since his death these beautiful pictures have attracted attention, and some of them have passed into the possession of those by whom they are properly appreciated. In that which graces this number there are slight defects, which we notice only because we are jealous of the fidelity of our work. The prominent figure in the foreground [the pursuing Indian] is a little too

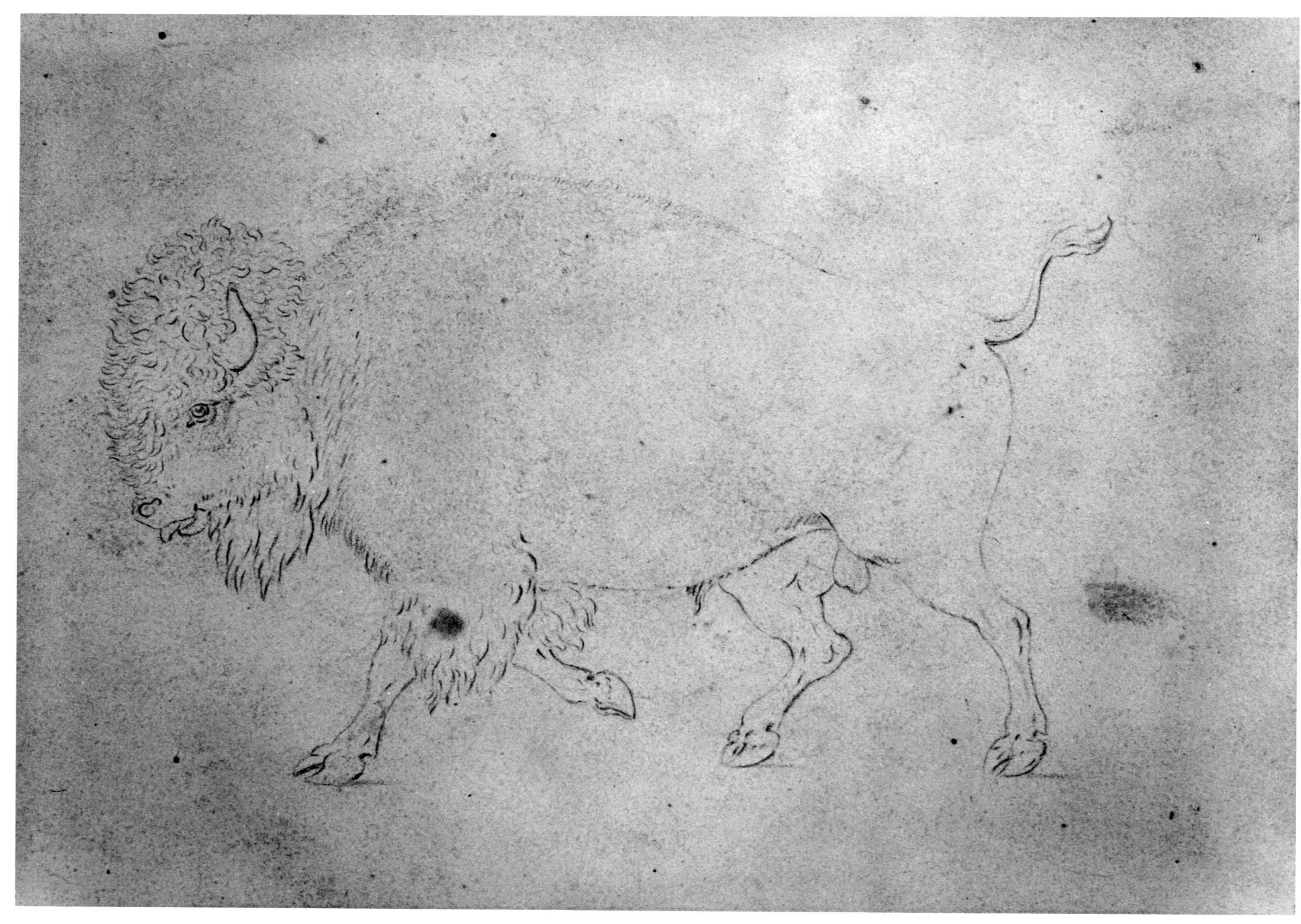

XXXIII. Bison [Untitled].
A sketch which probably served as a study for Rindisbacher's
buffalo hunting scenes painted in the 1830's.
Pencil, 8⅝ x 11 inches, ca. 1833.
Courtesy of Glenbow-Alberta Institute, Calgary.

much encumbered with drapery. The costume is correct in itself, but misplaced; and there is a slight inaccuracy in the mode in which the arrow is grasped by the right hand. All else is true to nature. The landscape and the animals are faithfully depicted; and the wild scene which is daily acted upon our prairies is placed vividly before the eye.[76]

Despite the minor flaws in the lithograph pointed out by McKenney and Hall, this picture too gained wide fame, and served as a model for many years for other artists who attempted to depict a plains Indian in close pursuit of a buffalo.

In the meantime, Peter had become a permanent resident of St. Louis. He had moved there from Fever River in 1829, probably late in the summer after the treaty council at Prairie du Chien.[77] Although he was only 23 years old, he had a reputation as a talented painter, and it is certain that his abilities were already known to some of the leading citizens in St. Louis, including those in civic, social, military and intellectual circles. In later years, Mrs. Fred G. Grisard, one of the Red River colonists who had migrated to Fever River and knew the Rindisbachers, wrote that when Peter went to St. Louis, "he was placed in a studio of a portrait painter of some note."[78] What this means is not clear. He may have been taken in by another painter, or shared quarters with him, but there is no record of the presence in St. Louis of any other resident artist of distinction during the time that Rindisbacher lived there.[79]

Mrs. Grisard also wrote that Peter's drawings attracted the attention of some U.S. army officers at St. Louis "who later took him with them on military excursions up the Missouri River."[80] We have no further information on those "excursions," but there is no doubt that Peter had already become friendly with a number of army officers on the Mississippi and, through them, may have met others in St. Louis. He was still young, virile, and adventurous, a manly youth who had been interested in the military life when he had been a boy in Switzerland; he had grown used to an existence of hardships and dangers; and he could draw the unusual scenes of his adventures. Among the friends he is known to have made, and who admired his work and were already becoming his patrons and publicists, were two officers at Jefferson Barracks, Captain Richard B. Mason and Lieutenant Reuben Holmes. Mason, a member of the First Infantry, later participated in the Black Hawk War, became a major in the First Dragoons, went to the Southwest with Stephen Watts Kearney during the Mexican War, became the first American military and civil governor of California, and sent back the first word of the discovery of gold in 1848 to President Polk. Holmes,

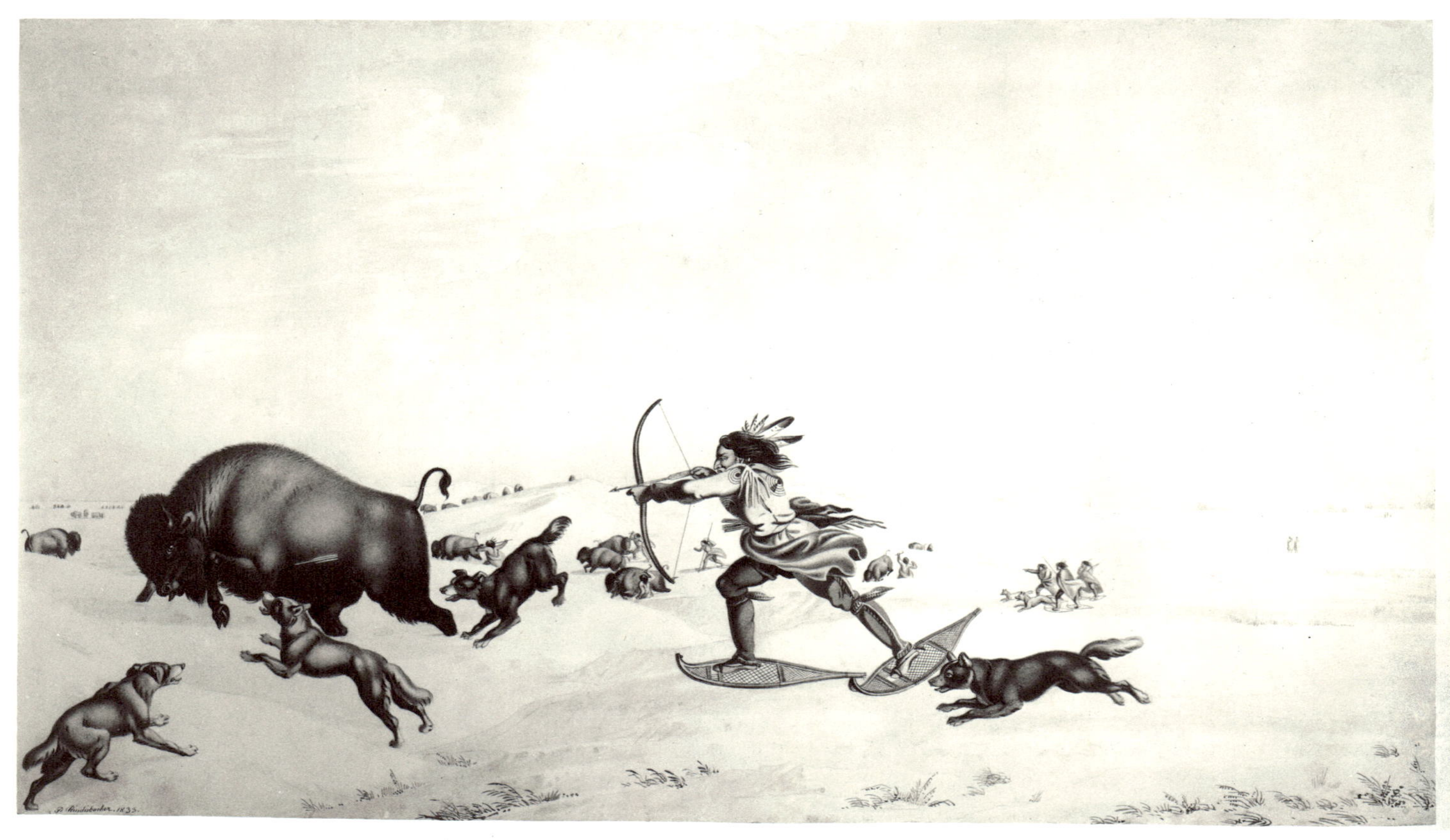

XXXIV. Blackfeet hunting on snowshoes [Untitled].
Watercolor, 9¼ x 15⅞ inches, 1833.
Collection of Amon Carter Museum, Fort Worth.

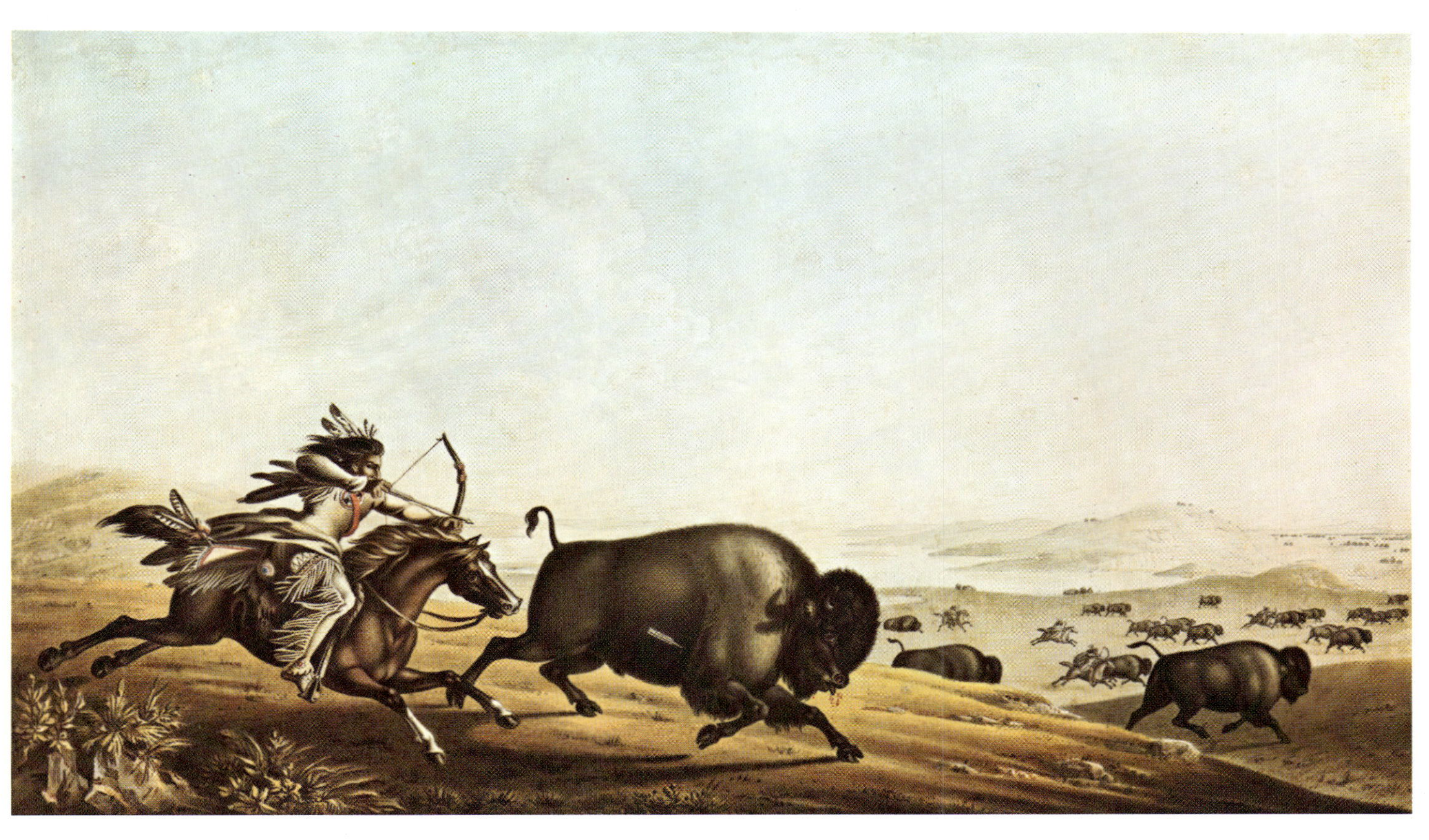

XXXV. Blackfeet hunting on horseback [Untitled].
Watercolor, 9¼ x 15⅞ inches, 1833.
Collection of Amon Carter Museum, Fort Worth.

a literary man, had mingled with fur traders during duty on the Missouri River and about 1828 had published "The Five Scalps," a biography of the fur trapper, Edward Rose, in the *St. Louis Beacon*. Later, as a captain, Holmes served in the Black Hawk War and died on November 4, 1833, at Jefferson Barracks, almost a year before Rindisbacher's death.

These officers, or others at St. Louis, went up the Missouri River from time to time, usually on missions to Fort Leavenworth, and on one or more occasions Peter may have accompanied them. At such times, he might have come on new subjects to paint, including the view portrayed in the McKenney and Hall "Buffalo Hunt." But he would have had to travel far beyond Fort Leavenworth for such a scene; the setting of that picture, in fact, suggests the Missouri River country in the Dakotas rather than Kansas.

Nevertheless, Holmes, Mason, and perhaps others, appear to have been busy on Peters' behalf even before he arrived in St. Louis. In the October, 1829, issue of a new periodical, *The American Turf Register and Sporting Magazine*, published in Baltimore, appeared one of his drawings, "Sioux Warrior Charging," as an illustration accompanying an article on "Horsemanship of the North American Indians." The drawing was apparently sent or taken East by one of Peter's friends, and the article's author, "Don Alphonso," named "Mr. Rindisbacker" as the artist. Three months later, in its January, 1830, issue, the magazine ran an article on the youth who had made the engraving of Rindisbacher's drawing, a deaf and dumb orphan boy named Albert Newsam, who worked for Colonel Childs. At the conclusion of its long story on Newsam, the editors added the note: "The original drawing, evincing talents of the first order, was made by P. Reindesbacker, a young Swiss, from Berne, who came to this country with Selkirk's fur company, about seven years since."

This journalistic salute to the lithographer, rather than to the artist, drew a response from an unknown correspondent, who may have been the same person who supplied the *Turf Register* with the original Rindisbacher drawing. In its February, 1830, issue, the periodical ran a letter written in Washington, D. C., on October 17, and printed in part in the *St. Louis Beacon* on December 12, 1829.[81] It stated that even though the lithograph was "certainly of no ordinary character . . . the original possesses yet greater claims to our admiration. It is a painting of nearly twice the size of the copy in the magazine; was taken from nature; and is remarkable for its spirit and the neatness of its execution. The artist, whose name is Rindisbacher, is a young man, and has lived since early youth in our *western wilds*. He is perfectly acquainted with the subject of his very successful effort; and has, the writer of this is informed, in his portfolio, views of many of the finest scenes in that part of the country, whose *untamed wilderness* has never before furnished subjects for the pencil or the burin. He has, however, more — a genius as fruitful, and an imagination as vivid as the scenes amongst which he has dwelt. These will enable him, in cultivating his fine talents, to throw aside the threadbare subjects of the schools, and give to the world themes as fresh as the soil upon which he was bred; — glowing as the newness of nature; and as picturesque as a combination of bold scenery, with bolder man and manners, will afford. I trust he will ere long be amongst us; when an enlightened public will not hesitate properly to appreciate him."[82]

The letter suggests that the writer, in Washington, had not yet met Rindisbacher, who was then still a resident of Gratiot's Grove, but had received his drawing and heard about him from someone else who had written or come from St. Louis.[83] The correspondent, nevertheless, was a man interested in the West and had an appreciation for the fact that Rindisbacher was making drawings of subjects that were new and novel and that no one else had yet drawn — subjects of the lands beyond the civilized regions of the United States, where Indians still roamed in "wildness" and freedom, and where men of urbanity and culture had not yet traveled. The artist was picturing, moreover, an area to which public attention was turning with increasing interest — the Mississippi Valley and beyond, which expansionist Americans were beginning to eye. In that sense, his drawings also had an element of "newsworthiness." Soon, that element of compelling allurement would draw Catlin and others to the West to paint Indians and write books about their adventures for the stay-at-homes; but Rindisbacher, as the *Turf Register* and its correspondents sensed, was a pioneer, illustrating dramatic aspects of a locale that had never before been pictured.

In July, 1830, the *Turf Register* carried a second Rindisbacher drawing, together with a letter from an officer at Jefferson Barracks, dated April 16, 1830, which was after Peter had moved to St. Louis. Addressed to the editor, it stated that "Mr. H [perhaps Reuben Holmes, who had possibly sent Peter's first drawing East] informs me that you are alive to the merits and promise of Mr. Rindisbacher" and went on to say that he now had the "great pleasure to introduce him yet more particularly . . . by a *pen drawing of a buffalo attacked by a band of prairie wolves* [published in the same number]. His familiarity with these subjects," the writer, whose name was not printed, continued, "the accuracy of their delineation, their freshness and novelty, give to him and his works an interest which few others can challenge. The generous anticipation of the Washington writer [an allusion to the letter writer of the previous October], that 'an enlightened public will not hesitate properly to appreciate him,' we feel assured will be most abundantly realized."

The writer went on to describe Rindisbacher as a "young artist, self-taught, and without advantage" and then discussed all the paintings, the originals and copies of the works which he had done in previous years in Canada and on the upper Mississippi, and which Peter had with him in St. Louis. "His port folio," the writer pointed out, "contains many fine efforts. The Indian dance [possibly the Sauk and Fox War Dance] is without fault; and, of itself, sufficient to establish a reputation. The buffalo chase [the subject of the McKenney and Hall lithograph perhaps] is pronounced true to nature, by all who can estimate its merits. He is very happy in his landscapes; and, when time and opportunities shall permit him to spread the magnifiicent west before the admirers of the grand and picturesque, his sketches from Hudson's bay to St. Louis, will, I have no doubt, secure him a lasting reputation."

Thereafter, the *Turf Register* continued to run Rindisbacher drawings. The February, 1832, issue contained a steel engraving by Hatch and Smillie of his picture of "Deer Hunting on the Water By Lamp Light," accompanied by an explanatory letter from a correspondent using the name Wah-o-pe-kah, and writing from the Missouri River country "Above Prairie Des Chiens."[84] Another Rindisbacher sketch, "Grouse of the Western and North Western Prairies," made into a lithograph by Colonel Childs and the artist Henry Inman, appeared in the August, 1832, issue. A note run with it announced that another Rindisbacher drawing of grouse of the southern region was being engraved by Oscar A. Lawson and would soon be published. In the October, 1832, issue, however, the Rindisbacher contribution was a dramatic scene of two woodlands Indians in a birchbark canoe hunting waterbirds in a setting of the Minnesota-Great Lakes wild rice-gathering region. An explanatory letter, signed only with the initial "R." (possibly Reuben Holmes or Richard Mason), and dated March, 1832, described the drawing, titled "Indians Gathering Wild Rice and Shooting Wild Fowl," and stated: "The drawing sent you by Mr. Rindisbacher, illustrating the method adopted by Indians to obtain the means of subsistence (for it does not refer alone to shooting), is applicable to all the Indians from the Lakes to the Mississippi."

The December, 1832, issue contained a picture of a prairie wolf "taken in the trap of the western hunter, who is represented in the plate,

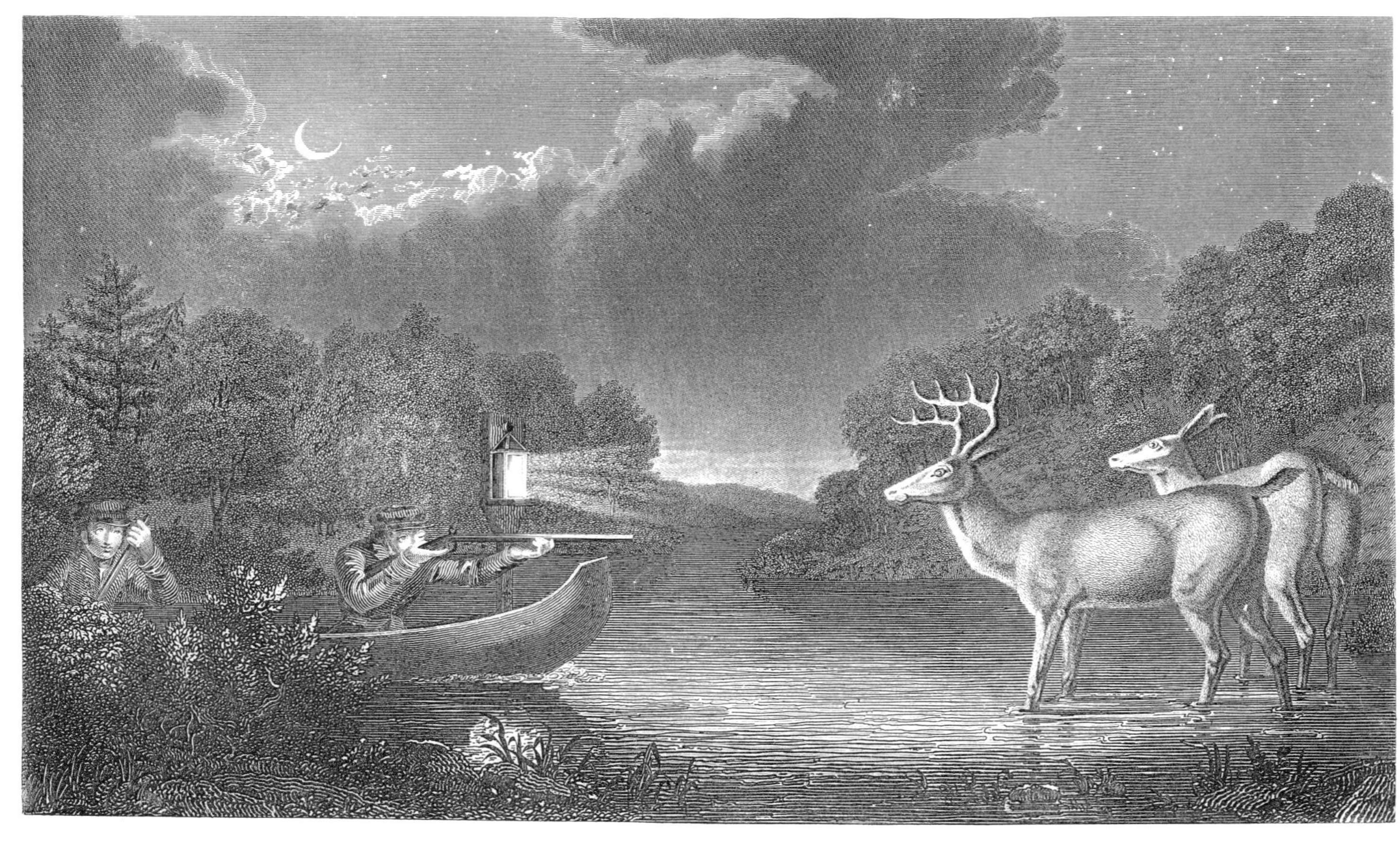

XXXVI. *Deer Hunting, Nocturnal and Aquatic.*
Steel engraving. [Size and date of original unknown].
American Turf Register and Sporting Magazine, Vol. 3 (February, 1832), facing page [257].

with his destroying club, approaching in the distance." The Rindisbacher work was stated this time as "another of the beautiful sketches, presented to the readers of this magazine by Captain Mason and Lieutenant Holmes, of the army" and was described as "another example of the fine tact of Mr. Rindisbacher, and, with various others in store, will afford to American, and more especially to European, readers, entertaining specimens of the game, and the modes of taking it, now almost peculiar to the western regions of America."

Although the periodical by then seems to have had in its possession several Rindisbacher works, possibly sent to it in a batch by "R." in March, 1832, some cause — perhaps the work of making lithographs of them — delayed their publication. In January, 1833, the magazine announced that it would soon publish "a beautiful drawing by Rindisbacher, representing Capt. Mason of the Army, in the act of shooting, *with one hand*, from on horseback, two deer crossing the Prairie — holding the reins in *one hand*, whilst he fired both barrels with the other — his horse being, as supposed, not practiced to stand fire." The lithograph, showing the mounted Mason in the background and two wounded deer falling in the foreground, finally appeared in the June, 1833, issue, accompanied by an article on " 'Bouncing Deer' in the 'American Bottom'," written by "R." in March, 1832.

The Black Hawk "War" had, meanwhile, occurred, and from April, 1832, until the final, grim massacre of Black Hawk's followers at the Bad Axe River on August 3, both Holmes and Mason had participated in the conflict. Whether Peter had accompanied his military friends during any part of the campaign against the Indians is not known. For a time, however, the hostilities raged somewhat near the vicinity of the Fever River settlements, occasioning the raising, again, of volunteer units of miners and settlers in that area, and it is possible that Peter had more than a curious observer's interest in the conflict. But there is no evidence, either in his known paintings or elsewhere, to indicate that he participated in any way in the Black Hawk affair.

The military excitement undoubtedly diverted his patrons' attention from sending more of his work to the East, but the *Turf Register* still possessed some paintings that had been sent to it previously, probably by "R." in March, 1832, and in August, 1833, the periodical ran the long-promised "Wilson's Pinnated Grouse" of the southern region. "For the drawing," it noted, "we are indebted, as for other valuable contributions, to Major Mason and Lieut. Holmes of the army of the United States; at whose instance Mr. Rindisbacher had the kindness to make the sketch for the American Turf Register and Sporting Magazine."

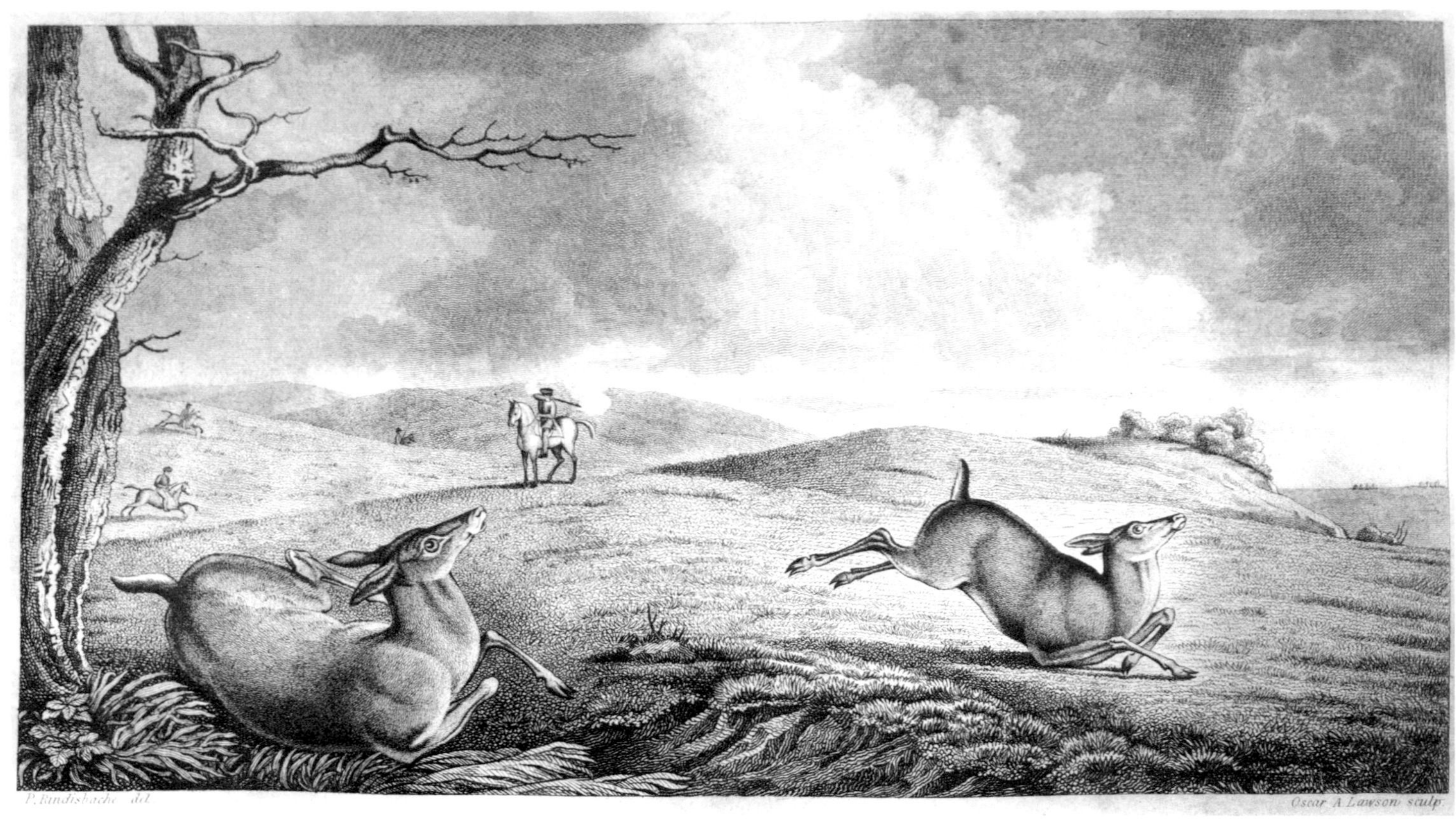

XXXVII. *Killing Two Deer with a Bird Gun.*
Steel engraving. [Size and date of original unknown].
American Turf Register and Sporting Magazine, Vol. 4 (June, 1833), facing page [531].

In October, 1833, the magazine ran a woodcut of a "Wild Turkey Trap," which the editors explained they had "selected from the inimitable drawings of our friend Rindisbacher." On November 4, Reuben Holmes, then 33 years old, died at Jefferson Barracks, but in its December issue, the *Turf Register* published a cut of another deer-hunting view by Rindisbacher, made in March, 1832, in the American Bottom opposite St. Louis, and depicting "the late Capt. Holmes, U.S.A.," shooting a deer. A letter, also written in March, 1832, and signed by "B.," explained that the writer, along "with several other gentlemen of St. Louis," had witnessed the hunt. This was the last Rindisbacher picture run by the *Turf Register* during the artist's lifetime, and indicates perhaps that, after March, 1832, it received no more examples of his work from his military friends in St. Louis.[85] In October, 1840, it did run one last Rindisbacher work, a drawing of an "American Hunter's Camp," which Theodore B. Skinner, the son of a former editor of the magazine, found in his possession and gave to the periodical.[86]

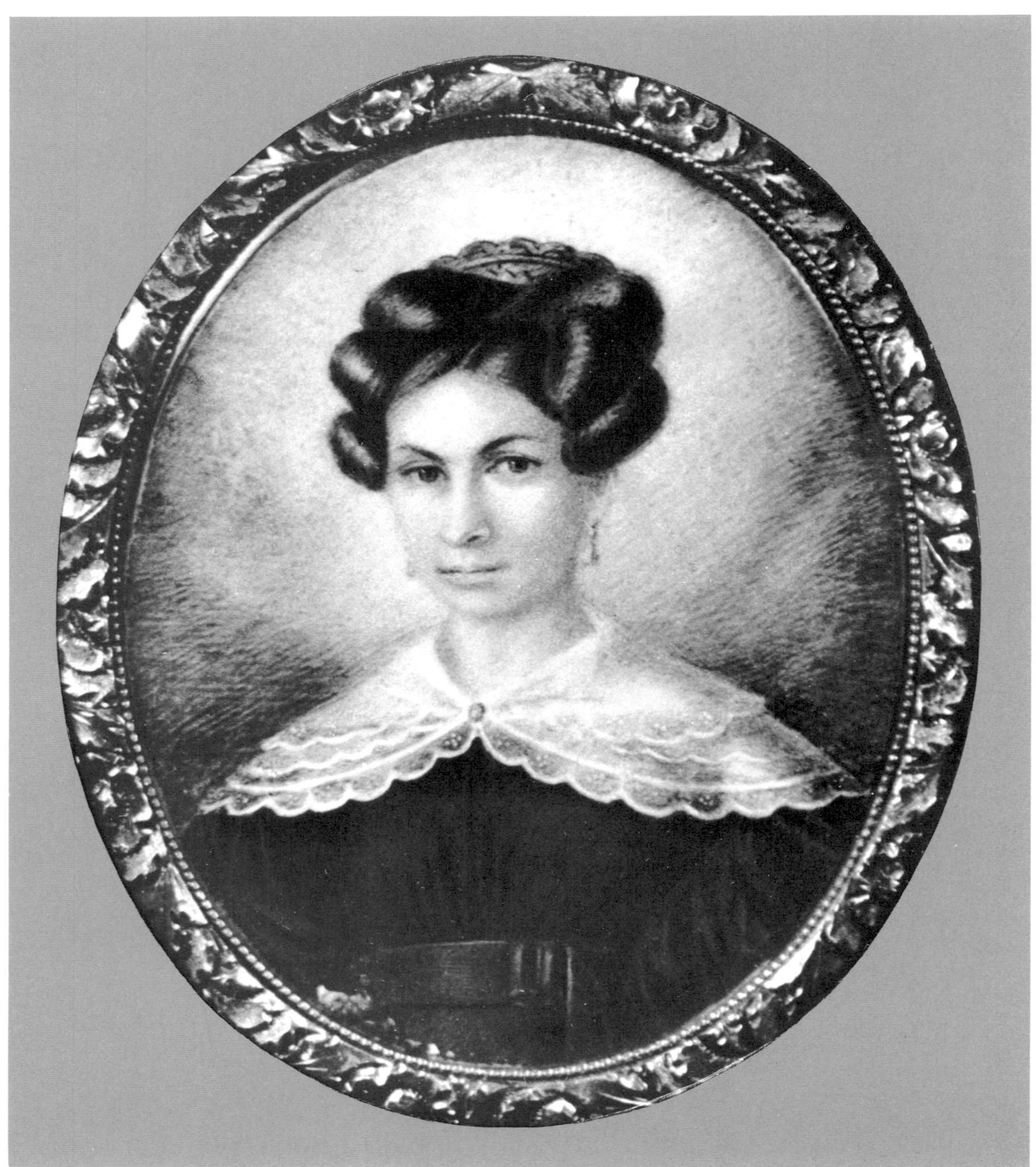

XXXVIII. Victorine A. Barronsell Tesson (1793–1869) [Untitled].
Watercolor on ivory, 2¼ x 1¼ inches, 1830.
Courtesy of Louis T. Hall, Jr., El Dorado, Arkansas;

V. ST. LOUIS: THE LAST YEARS

During the five years that Rindisbacher lived in St. Louis, he did considerably more than the works represented in the *Turf Register*. As early as December 12, 1829, soon after his arrival in the city, the *St. Louis Beacon* ran a letter, which Peter's friend "R." had written to it five days earlier. Addressed to Messrs. Keemle & Brooks of the paper, it read:

> *Gentlemen* — I have this morning amused myself in the examination of Mr. Rindisbacher's port-folio. I am afraid it is not generally known that this artist now resides in this city, engaged in sketching from nature, taking miniature portraits and copying occasionally from engravings. Mr. Rindisbacher has marked out a new track, and almost invented a new style of painting — one, too, of much interest. His sketches of groups or single Indians, are deserving of the highest admiration. The proportions and development of muscle, in his delineations of the human figure, are extremely correct. There is a living and moving effect in the swell and contraction he gives to the muscular appearance of his figures, that evinces much observation, judgment and skill. Talent, I might almost say genius, like his, deserves encouragement, and, undoubtedly, were he in a place of more fashion and leisure, he would receive it. Those who have not yet examined his fine paintings of Indian dances, lodges, &c. will be well paid for their trouble by calling at his rooms and viewing a style of painting so new and novel.

Mention has been made of the collection of eighteen Rindisbacher watercolors in the West Point Museum. Although they are copies of earlier paintings, they are considered among the finest work Rindisbacher ever did, reflecting his matured abilities as an artist, and it is thought therefore that he must have done them in St. Louis in the last years of his life. But the references in the December, 1829, letter to his unusual delineation of the muscular features of the human body might well be applied also to the West Point paintings and would seem to indicate that, if he had not already made those copies, he was, indeed, developing the style which they exhibit.

In addition to his sporting scenes and copies of his earlier paintings, which he seems to have made from time to time as demand for one or more of them arose, Peter executed in St. Louis, on order, an unknown number of miniature portraits, some of them done on ivory. As stated earlier, he seems to have had a reputation as a portraitist while he still lived at Gratiot's Grove, and although several examples of his small portraits done in that region are known, it is possible that many more will eventually turn up among family possessions. In St. Louis, where he had painted Mr. Hempstead in June, 1829, he continued to receive commissions after he became a permanent resident. In 1830 a Mrs. Coralie Tesson Polkowski is known to have sat for him.[87] On April 30, 1831, Peter advertised in the *St. Louis Times* that he would execute "MINIATURE AND LANDSCAPE PAINTINGS, &c. on the most reasonable terms" at his work room on Locust Street between Main and Second. He added that "His stay in this place is limited to the ensuing fall," although this might have been a "scare" advertising tactic rather than a true intention, for it is not known that he did leave St. Louis that fall.

Perhaps the ad brought him further business. It cannot be guessed how many commissions he executed between 1831 and 1834, when he died, for all of his work will never be found. But among his portraits that have been noted, at one time or another, are one of a "Lady Ruthven," which was shown in the Mechanics Fair at St. Louis in November, 1842;[88] two "small bust portraits in pencil of Phillipe Frederic and Eugenie Schirmer, attributed to Peter Rindisbacher, whose sister was the wife of Mrs. Schirmer's brother, Charles Monnier";[89] and a miniature painting of the son of a Mrs. Moore, to whom Peter wrote on June 27, 1832, requesting a payment of $2.00 for the portrait — an indication, perhaps, of what the artist had meant when he had advertised "the most reasonable terms."[90]

By the early 1830's people who were interested in the Plains Indians and frontier life beyond the Mississippi were turning up in St. Louis, and it is probable that authorities on the Indians in that city, like General William Clark, the celebrated explorer who was then Superintendent of Indian Affairs, were telling them to see Rindisbacher's paintings.[91] We have no record of all those who called on Peter, but among them may have been Prince Maximilian of Weid, who arrived in St. Louis in

March, 1833, with the Swiss-born artist, Karl Bodmer. Maximilian and his party started up the Missouri River in April of that year and returned to St. Louis in May, 1834. Either before or after the trip, Maximilian, perhaps accompanied by Bodmer, may have called on the other Swiss artist, resident in St. Louis, and bought some paintings from him, for two Rindisbacher watercolors and a wash drawing were found in the Prince's personal collection in the 1950's.[92] In 1834, also, Peter was visited by Charles Fenno Hoffman of New York, who was also interested in Plains Indian life. After viewing Peter's paintings, Hoffman wrote: "They [the Indian horsemen depicted in Peter's works] would take the eye of a painter; and have, in fact, suggested some most spirited sketches to Rindisbacher, a highly original artist at St. Louis, at whose rooms I have spent more than one agreeable hour."[93]

Little information has been found concerning Peter's sudden death in 1834. That year he was among the signers of the constitution of the St. Louis Grays, a volunteer military unit, of which he must have been a founding member. The Minute Book of the Grays carries the following notations about Rindisbacher in a section devoted to individual accounts:

> 1834 Aug 9 meeting .50 Aug[t] 12th Died this day and buried
> due .25 by the C° 13th.[94]

The cause of the artist's sudden and premature death, at the age of 28, is unknown. It has been guessed by some that he was the victim of cholera; others tend to believe that, if it was cholera, he would have been too ill from the symptoms to have been able to attend the meeting of the Grays on August 9.[95]

On August 15, the *Missouri Republican* of St. Louis carried the following obituary notice:

> DIED — On the 13th inst., Mr. P. Rindisbacher, Miniature and Landscape Painter.[96]

> Mr. Rindisbacher had talents which gave every assurance of future celebrity. He was generally known by his graphic sketches of Indian life, some of which, engraved for the Sporting Magazine, have excited much attention. He was much beloved for his many virtues; he possessed a keen sensibility and the most delicate perception of the beautiful. But alas!

> "No more for him the scenes he loved so well
>   Will gleam in beauty on the ravished sight;
> The woodland's shade — the prairies sunny swell —
>   The glowing noontide — and the solemn night;

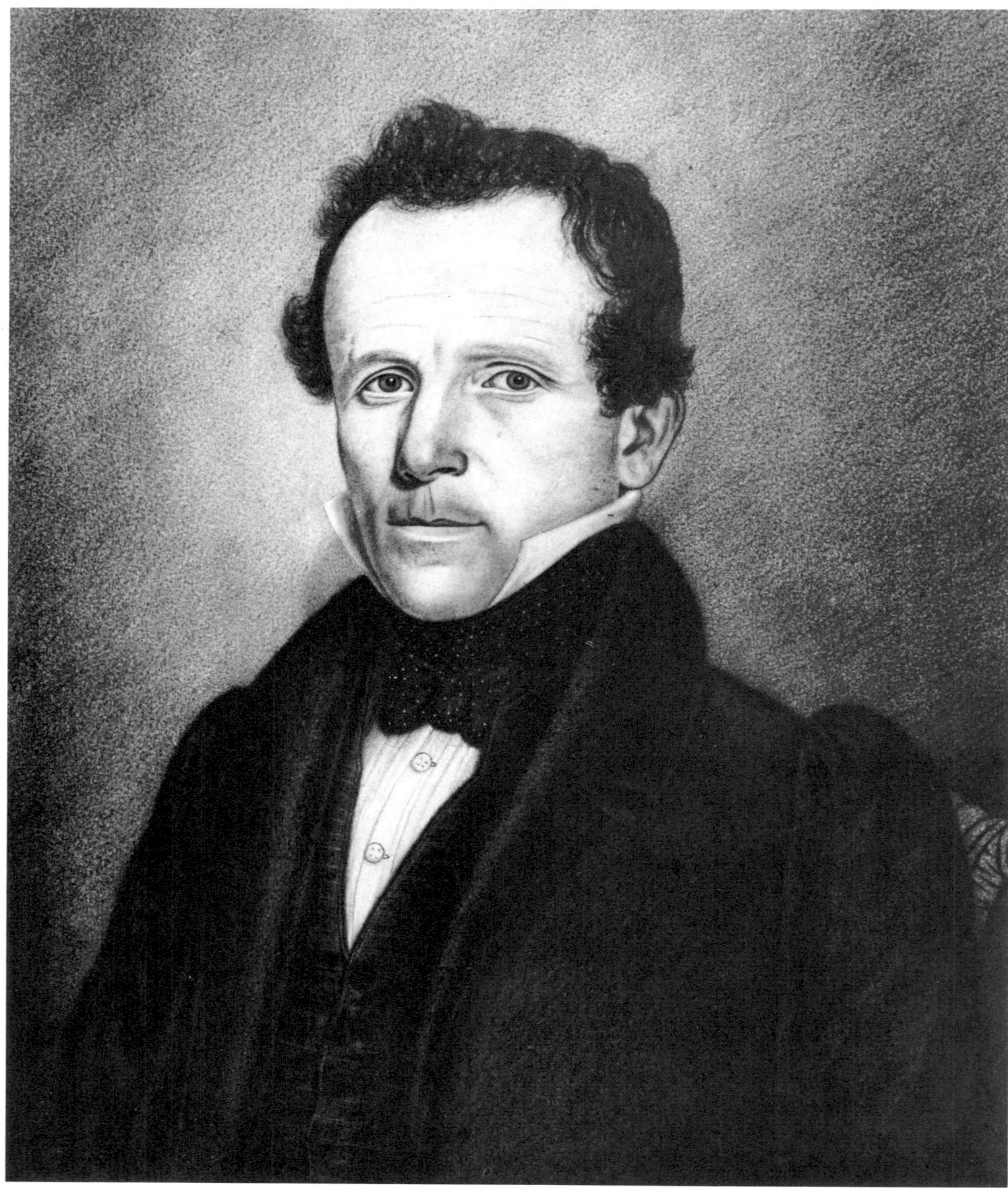

XXXIX. Mr. Philippe Schirmer (1799–1850) [Untitled].
Crayon on paper, 12 x 10 inches, ca. 1832.
Courtesy of the Missouri Historical Society, St. Louis.

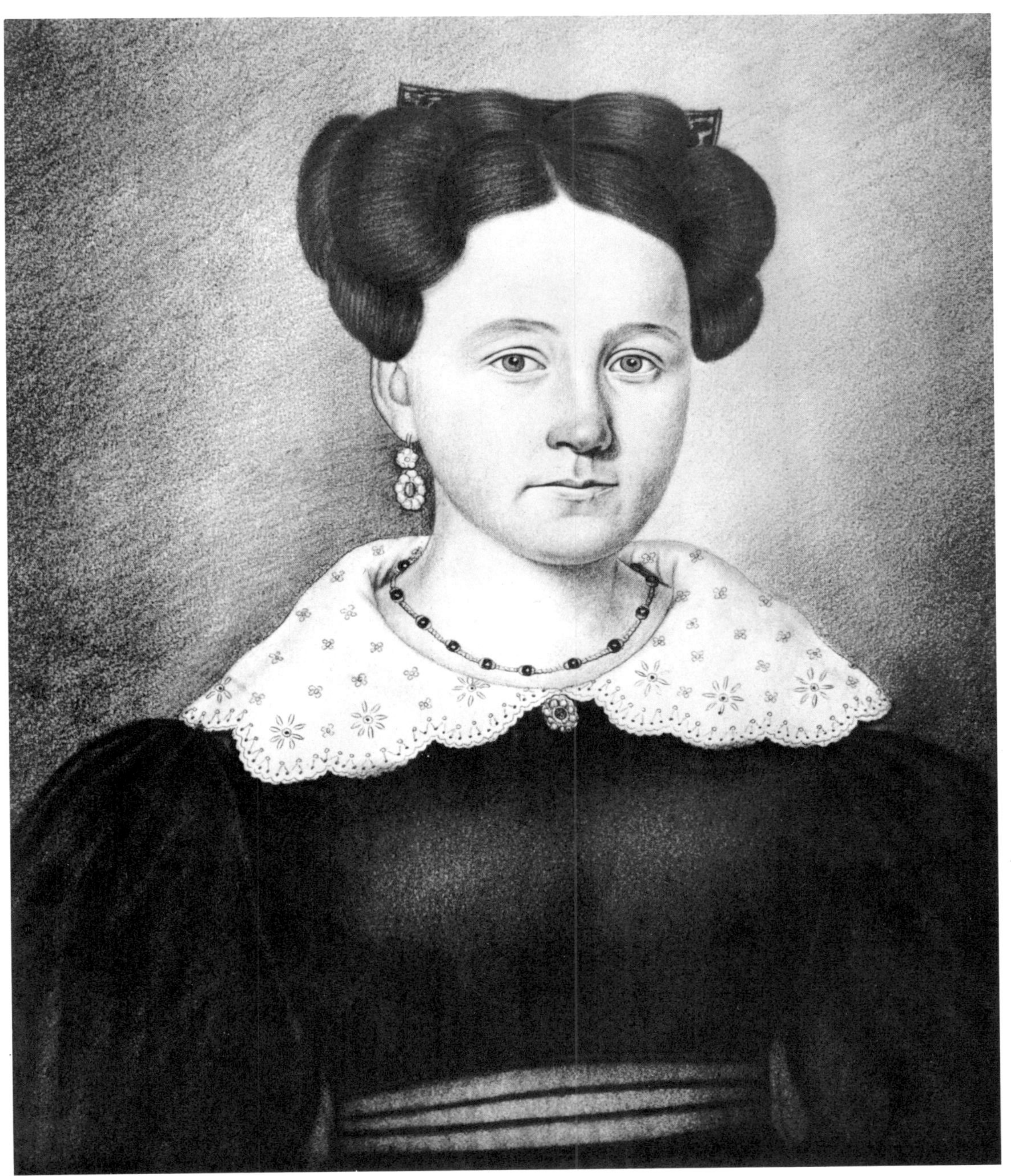

XL. Mrs. Philippe (Eugenie Monnier) Schirmer [Untitled].
Crayon on paper, 12 x 10 inches, ca. 1832.
Courtesy of the Missouri Historical Society, St. Louis.

> "No more will these, or aught of nature's store,
>   With joy, to Genius known, his busom fill.
>   The heartfelt throb — the flush his high brow o'er —
>   The blood's quick rush — the fitful pleasing thrill!
>
> "All's quiet now! calm, passionless, and cold!
>   But the warm heart's poor tenant's upward fled;
> In brighter scenes to taste of joy untold,
>   And join the circle of th' illustrious dead!"

Where the members of his company of St. Louis Grays buried the young artist, probably with military honors, is also not known. Peter's father seems to have taken possession of his drawings and paintings, some of which he later distributed, or left, to various other members of of the family.[97] At least one person was particularly interested in acquiring the works that Peter left. Many years later, on April 13 and 14, 1870, the *Neue Zürcher Zeitung* in Zurich published an article in German which it said it had taken from an American paper, explaining that "although it deals with one who died some time ago, its publication in our paper is nevertheless justified because it deals with an important Swiss artist who is almost completely forgotten in his native land." The article, titled "Rindisbacher, the Painter," was signed by "F.M.," whose identity has never been established, and it is not known when and where the article was originally published in America. It is probable, however, that it appeared initially in an English or German newspaper published in St. Louis long after Rindisbacher's death, since it refers to St. Louis as having had a smaller German population "in Rindisbacher's time" than when the article was published and states that "several European painters already have made sketches of some of Rindisbacher's works and probably will publish them in their native lands under their own names." Of considerable interest, however, is the information it conveys about a "Major Hughes of Washington," whom it does not otherwise identify. "As soon as he [Hughes] was informed of the death of the young artist," the article states, "he inquired into his life history and subsequently made an effort to obtain the works remaining in his studio. For these Hughes generously paid the heirs a considerable sum. So it is that Rindisbacher's most interesting paintings are owned by this man."[98] All efforts to discover the identity of this "Major Hughes" have so far failed, but it has been suggested that he may have been the original purchaser of the Rindisbacher collection that is now at West Point.

The articles republished in the *Neue Zürcher Zeitung* were essentially a biography of the artist, based on the information gathered by "Major

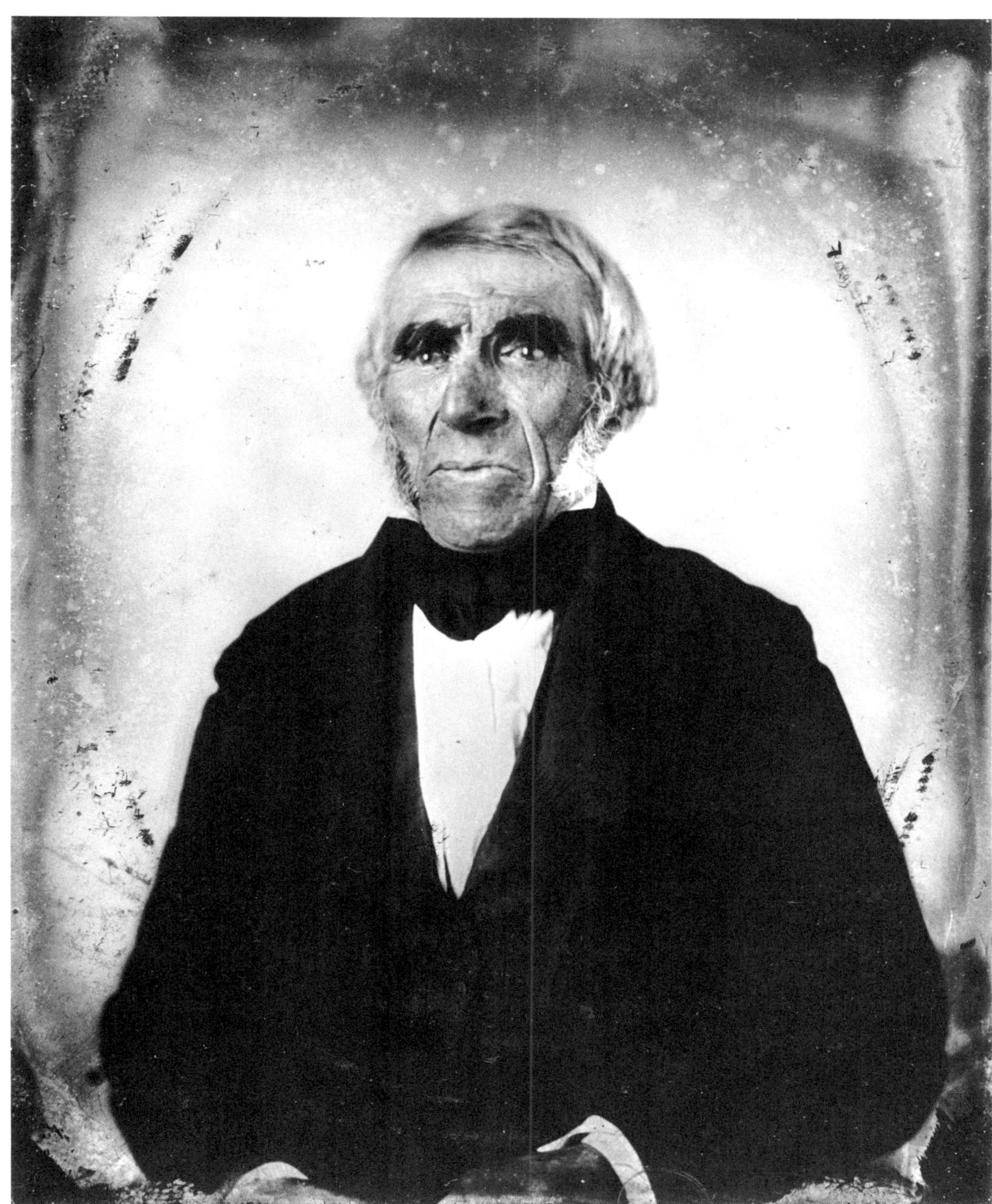

XLI. Pierre Rindesbacher [Untitled].
The artist's father accumulated many of his son's works,
which have remained in the hands of the family ever since.
Tintype, 4¼ x 3¼ inches, ca. 1864/1865.
Courtesy of Mrs. Chloe Rindesbacher Smith, Stockton, Illinois.

Hughes" while he was inquiring into Peter's life soon after his death. By the time of the articles' publication in 1870 in Switzerland, Rindisbacher, as the editor noted, had been almost completely forgotten in his original homeland. The same could have been said about him in America. Nor did the 1870 biography rekindle interest in him in either country. The first artist to paint the West of Canada and the spirited life of the unconquered Indians of the great plains remained obscure, forgotten by all save a handful of specialists, a situation that has continued with little change even until the present day.

NOTES

1) Some present-day descendants of the artist's brothers and sisters state that his full name was Peter Francis Rindisbacher and that the family always referred to him as Francis. (Letter from Mrs. Elizabeth Eames, a descendant of Peter's brother, Frederic, to Mitchell Wilder, Amon Carter Museum, May 5, 1969). Mrs. Eames made this statement after interviewing other family members in Illinois and Wisconsin in the spring of 1969, but added: "However, elsewhere he was known as Peter." The statement may be correct. But the author has found no documentary evidence to corroborate his having been given the name Peter Francis, nor has he come upon a single written reference to him as Francis by anyone during, or after, his lifetime.

2) See "Peter Rindisbacher, der Indianermaler aus dem Emmental" ("Peter Rindisbacher, The Indian Painter from Emmenthal") by Karl Meuli in *Beiträge zur Volkskunde* of the University of Basel, Basel, Switzerland, 1960, pp. 140-175. I used a translation of this interesting and informative study of Rindisbacher made by Bert Wetanson and kindly provided to me by Mrs. Elizabeth Eames. In discussing Catlin's error, Meuli cites "George Catlin, Painter of Indians and the West" by John C. Ewers in the *Annual Report of the Smithsonian Institution for 1955*, Washington, D.C., 1956, p. 500. The picture in question may be seen in Catlin's *Letters and Notes on the Manners, Customs, and Condition of the North American Indians*, New York, 1842, Vol. I, Plate 109, opp. p. 254.

3) In my bibliography I have cited the many works that have been of assistance to me. But a number of persons, including the authors of some of those works, deserve a special note of appreciation and gratitude for the contributions their research made to this study. They include Dr. Grace Lee Nute, whose writings first began to arouse interest in Rindisbacher in the 1930's; Margaret Arnett MacLeod and Clifford P. Wilson, who provided more information on the artist in the 1940's; John Francis McDermott, who added much new material in 1949; the late Karl Meuli, whose 1960 article has already been mentioned; and Mrs. Elizabeth Eames, who did considerable research for this study and unselfishly provided her findings to the author. To them especially, but also to others who are listed in the bibliography, I extend my thanks, as well as my acknowledgment that this study, to a large extent, rests on their pioneering work.

4) The Rindisbacher children were: Elizabeth, baptised February 2, 1801; Christian, born October 9, 1803; Peter born April 12, 1806; Anna Barbara, born October 2, 1808; Christina, born February 20, 1811; Magdalena, born September 27, 1812; and Verena, born June 20, 1815. Another son, Frederic, was born at Red River in 1822. This information, and much of the material on Peter's ancestry and youth, comes from Meuli, who drew, for many of his particulars, on records in Switzerland. Other information on Peter's early years may be found in "Peter Rindisbacher, Swiss Artist" in *Minnesota History*, Vol. 32 (September, 1951), pp. 155-162. The latter is a translation by Anna M. Heilmaier, with an introduction by Michel Benisovich, of two articles on "Rindisbacher, the Painter" that appeared in the *Neue Zürcher Zeitung*, Zurich, Switzerland, April 13 and 14, 1870, signed only by "F.M." and stemming from inquiries about the artist's life made soon after Rindisbacher's death in 1834 by a "Major Hughes" of Washington, D.C. Nothing is known of the identity of either "F.M." or "Major Hughes."

5) A pencil drawing, with color, it is owned today by the Glenbow-Alberta Institute in Calgary, Alberta.

6) Meuli, n. 60. Switzerland at the time, it should be noted, was experiencing social and political turmoil as well as periods of famine. Many Swiss were dissatisfied with conditions, and Peter Sr.'s restlessness may have stemmed as much from the stress of the times as from his temperament.

7) For the pertinent facts concerning Selkirk's colony see *Hudson's Bay Company, 1670-1870* by E. E. Rich, Hudson's Bay Record Society, London, Vol. II, 1959, pp. 288-332, 426, 428-429, 507-508. Also, *The Red River Valley, 1811-1849: a regional study* by John P. Pritchett, Yale University Press, New Haven, 1942.

8) Von May spoke French, German, Italian and English with "decided fluency" (Pritchett, p. 224). The French-speaking colonists knew him as Rodolphe de May, and some accounts refer to him as du May.

9) Von May's recruiting pamphlet, printed in Berne in 1820, was titled "Brief and True Account of All the Advantages A Colonist in the Red River Colony Located in North America May Expect and Enjoy."

10) *The Red River Colony* by Augustus L. Chetlain, Chicago, 1893, p. 35, quoting a letter from Mrs. Fred G. Grisard, a Red River colonist. The memory of Peter Sr. having been a leader may have reflected the fact that he was one of the few colonists who had a knowledge of farming and husbandry. This, combined with his "forceful" nature, may have caused the other families to look to him for leadership.

11) The passport document, issued to the emigrants by the authorities at Berne on May 3, 1821, lists the heads of families, enumerates the number of persons in each family, and adds them up for a total of 165 people. However, it lists Philippe Schirmer twice; totes up the "Pierre Rindisbacher" family as seven instead of eight; omits the name of Ludwig Engel, who was one of the emigrants; and in several other particulars seems unreliable as an exact count of the number of persons who actually departed from Berne. It is printed in George Bryce and C. N. Bell, "Original Letters and Other Documents Relating to the Selkirk Settlement . . ." The Historical and Scientific Society of Manitoba, *Transactions No. 33*, Winnipeg, 1889, p. 5 ff.

12) Meuli, p. 149.

13) "The Red River Colony" by A. L. Chetlain, *Harper's New Monthly Magazine*, Vol. 58 (December, 1878), p. 49. This article contains an engraving, probably made from a tintype, of Peter Rindisbacher Sr. in his old age.

14) Pritchett, p. 224.

15) Meuli, who first publicized this letter, credits its discovery in the *Berne Weekly* to Mr. Alfred Bartschi of Burgdorf, Switzerland, "who at my request looked through all the documents in Eggiwil and many others as well."

16) Augustus Louis Chetlain, born in St. Louis on December 26, 1824, served as a General on the staff of U. S. Grant in the Civil War. Besides his writings on the Red River Colony, cited above in notes 10 and 13, he published *Recollections of Seventy Years*, Galena, Ill., 1899. His father, whose name was spelled Chatelain in Switzerland, married Julia Droz, the daughter of another member of the Swiss emigrating party. The Chetlains left the Red River in 1823, migrated to St. Louis, and in 1826 moved to Galena, where the elder Chetlain engaged in mining and teaming, and later bought a farm.

17) Chetlain, *Harper's New Monthly Magazine*, p. 49.

18) Mrs. Grisard in Chetlain, *Red River Colony*, 1893, p. 35.

19) Later, he made watercolor copies of these sketches.

20) "Captain Lyon in the Arctic" by Thomas Dunbabin, *The Beaver*, Spring, 1963, p. 46. The surgeon, who did the marrying, may have been Dr. Louis Jacques Ostertag, who later became the husband of Peter's sister, Anna Barbara.

21) These Crees, who hunted in the watery country north and south of York Factory, were known as Maskegons, people of the muskeg or swamps. The whites referred to them as Swampy Crees.

22) "John West, Peguis and P. Rindisbacher" by Harry Shave, *The Beaver*, Summer, 1957, p. 17.

23) These Chippewas were known also as Salteaux Indians, a name given them originally by French-speaking fur men who had originally found many of their bands living about the rapids at present-day Sault Ste. Marie between Lakes Huron and Superior. Their own name for themselves, Ojibwa, had been corrupted into Chippewa by the English.

24) Immediately upon their arrival at Red River, the colonists were lodged in tents near Fort Douglas. After plans were made for the winter, those who stayed at Fort Douglas were taken into various homes of the de Meurons and others who were already settled at the colony. Those who went to Pembina built cabins for themselves or found what shelter they could with traders, hunters and others who were living in that area. Pritchett, p. 225.

25) The long drives of cattle and sheep from the United States to the Red River Colony in those early days is an interesting, but little known, part of the story of the livestock industry in America. Selkirk made many efforts to procure stock for the settlers, and he and the governors of the colony entered into a series of contracts for the delivery of cattle as well as sheep. About 1819, the first cattle arrived when British traders managed to drive a few head from Sault Ste. Marie through U. S. Indian lands to Red River. In 1820 officials at the colony contracted with Hercules L. Dousman, a fur trader and enterprising merchant at Prairie du Chien, to drive more cattle north. Dousman got a herd together at Prairie du Chien, but they starved there during the winter, and none reached the colony. In August, 1821, Joseph Rolette, a onetime Nor'Wester, and Alexis Bailly an agent of

the American Fur Company, fulfilling a contract made with Selkirk, finally reached the colony with a herd that had been driven north from Missouri, and sold the animals for $100 and more a head. A second attempt by Dousman failed the same year; Dousman got his cattle only as far as Lake Traverse that year. Later, sheep and cattle were driven successfully to the colony from Missouri, Louisiana, Wisconsin, and even Kentucky. See Pritchett, p. 252, and William W. Folwell, *A History of Minnesota*, Vol. I, Minnesota Historical Society, St. Paul, 1921, p. 216.

26) Chetlain, *Harper's New Monthly Magazine*, p. 51. "Early Days at Red River Settlement, and Fort Snelling . . ." reminiscences by Mrs. Ann Adams (Barbara Ann Scheidecker), one of the Swiss emigrants, published in the Minnesota Historical Society *Collections*, Vol. 6 (1894), pp. 75-115, repeats this, and considerable other information, in the exact words first published by Chetlain sixteen years earlier. Mrs. Adams' account, however, includes much additional material.

27) "Peter Rindisbacher, Red River Artist — Part I" by Margaret Arnett MacLeod, *The Beaver*, December, 1945, p. 32.

28) Frederick Merk, *Fur Trade and Empire*, Cambridge, Mass., 1931, pp. 179-180.

29) Frederic was born in 1822 and was baptized by the Reverend John West on October 30 of that year in the new Anglican church at Red River.

30) Many of the Swiss, including possibly the Rindisbachers, settled among the de Meurons along the Seine River, a small tributary that emptied into the Red River near Fort Douglas. Rindisbacher made several paintings of the confluence of the two rivers.

31) On August 4, 1822, the Colony's Governor described Fort Douglas as "the most filthy miserable place imaginable. It is, by at least 25 feet, too small, and the stockades are for the most part rotten and tumbling down. The buildings, except one, are mere log huts, very old and so full of holes as to be perfectly unsuitable." In 1825 Fort Douglas was sold, and the Governor of the Colony also moved to Fort Garry.

32) In 1822, an official report on the various settlers to the Governor of the Colony described the Rindisbacher family as follows: "Rindisbacher, Pierre, 41, born Lauperswyl

[a Swiss district], a Canton of Berne, veterinary surgeon, character good but not steady; wife Barbe, 37, character fair; sons, Chretien, 18, character fair; Pierre, 15, draughtsman, character good; Gautier, 2, adopted; daughters, Anne Barbe, 13, Chretienne, 10, Madeleine, 6, Verene, 4; religion, Reformed Church." MacLeod, *Beaver*, December, 1945, p. 31.

33) Rich, *Hudson's Bay Company*, Vol. II, p. 417.

34) "Peter Rindisbacher, Swiss Artist," *Minnesota History*, Vol. 32 (September, 1951), p. 156 (article from 1870 *Neue Zürcher Zeitung*, cited in note 4, above). The same source says: "Later he worked also in oils where specifically required, but we do not believe that any important work by him exists in this medium." Because Peter worked with watercolors, most of his works are, considering their meticulousness and the wealth of detail he included in them, surprisingly small. Many of them are no larger than approximately 6 inches by 8 inches — truly miniature gems.

35) "Rindisbacher, The Painter," *Neue Zürcher Zeitung*, April 13, 1870. Here, I have used Wetanson's translation of the text as it appeared in Meuli's article in *Beiträge zur Volkskunde*, cited above in note 2. Heilmaier gives a slightly different translation in *Minnesota History*, Vol. 32 (September, 1951), pp. 157, 159.

36) *Minnesota History*, September, 1951, p. 161. Margaret A. MacLeod in "The Company in Winnipeg," *The Beaver*, September, 1940, p. 7, noted that the Hudson's Bay Company's books "recorded a payment of 'six pounds nineteen shillings sterling'" for paintings of the Colony by Rindisbacher.

37) See *Wisconsin Magazine of History*, The State Historical Society of Wisconsin, Vol. 46, No. 1 (Autumn 1962), p. 15.

38) "Peter Rindisbacher, Red River Artist — Part III" by Clifford Wilson, *The Beaver*, December, 1945, p. 36.

39) The full title: *Views in Hudson's Bay. Taken by a Gentleman on the Spot in the Years, 1823 and 1824. Illustrative of the Customs, Manners and Costumes of those Tribes of North American Indians Amongst whom Capt'n. Franklin has passed in his present and former arduous undertaking.*

40) Wilson, *Beaver*, December, 1945, p. 35.

41) As a clerk, Peter may have worked for Hargrave.

42) Wilson, *Beaver*, December, 1945, p. 32, reprinted with the kind permission of the Champlain Society.

43) *Ibid*.

44) *Ibid*.

45) *Ibid*, p. 33.

46) Chetlain, *Harper's New Monthly Magazine*, pp. 53-54.

47) This account of the Tully episode is taken from Robert Campbell's unpublished manuscript reminiscences, entitled "Account of the early settlement of the Red River of the Privations, hardships and Sufferings of the first Settlers &c. — by one who was there," written in 1892 and made available to me through the kindness of Lucile M. Kane, Curator of Manuscripts, Minnesota Historical Society. Campbell and his family left Red River with the Tullys.

48) From Campbell's reminiscences.

49) A number of the families remained as "squatters" on the military reservation grounds at Fort St. Anthony for a year or more, and some settled there permanently.

50) "Mrs. Adéle P. Gratiot's Narrative" in *Wisconsin State Historical Collections*, Vol. X (1883-1885), pp. 261-275.

51) The Fever River had received its name from French fur trappers because of a smallpox epidemic that had once raged among Indians residing along its banks.

52) "Mrs. Gratiot's Narrative," p. 267. In the 1830's, after the Rindisbachers arrived in the United States, Peter Sr. changed the spelling of the family name to "Rindesbacher" because so many of his neighbors, including clerks and other officials, spelled it that way. The artist, however, always spelled it "Rindisbacher."

53) See "The Record Flood of 1826" by Francis Heron, with Introduction by Clifford Wilson, in *The Beaver*, September, 1950, pp. 42-46. An unfinished pencil sketch of the flood by Rindisbacher, showing the Anglican church and other buildings of the colony standing amid the high water, was reproduced in *The Beaver*, March, 1952, on the Contents page. Similar disastrous floods also struck the valleys of the St. Peter's, the Mississippi, and other rivers in that part of the continent that same year.

54) Altogether, 243 persons, mostly Swiss and de Meurons, left the Colony for the United States in 1826. See Folwell, *A History of Minnesota*, Vol. I, p. 217. Many of them seem to have preceded the Rindisbacher party and to have reached Fort Snelling by mid-July. On July 16 of that year, Benjamin F. Baker, a fur trader at the fort, wrote to local Indian agent, Major Lawrence Taliaferro, as follows: "These people that come from Red River have lodged about a hundred head of Cattle in the Bottom where we had inclosed for our stock and destroying the Pasture — I wish you would direct them to move them over on the opposite side of the Mississippi." Lawrence Taliaferro Papers, Minnesota Historical Society.

55) Chetlain, *Harper's New Monthly Magazine*, p. 55.

56) In the beginning, they farmed "on shares."

57) Peter's contacts with, and sales to, members of the U.S. Army during his 1826 trip to the Fever River district is, of course, conjecture. Moreover, it should be noted that Fort Crawford might have been empty when the Rindisbacher party passed it. It was badly damaged by floodwaters and was temporarily evacuated in October, 1826.

58) The great number of paintings that he had done, and sold, during his residence at Red River were now a legacy of the part of his life that he had left behind him. They were already scattered among purchasers at Red River, at various Hudson's Bay Company posts in Canada, and in England. In the twentieth century many of those paintings would appear at sales and be bought for private collections and for those at the Public Archives of Canada and other institutions. At least four of the works he did in Canada may include representations of himself. One, a sketch done in 1823 when Peter was seventeen, shows two young men shooting at quail, and is titled, "The artist and a young friend shooting quail with rifles." A second picture, also done about 1823, and owned today by the Peabody Museum at Harvard, is a watercolor titled "Inside of an Indian Tent." It is believed that it shows Peter himself sitting inside a tipi conversing with a group of Indians. The third, "Colonists on the Red River in North America," is an ink sketch done in 1825 and depicts a group of colonists inside one of their homes. An inscription on the reverse side of the drawing identifies the people in the drawing as "1.2. Swiss colonist

with Wife and Children from the Canton Bern [probably Peter's Father, Mother, his four-year-old sister Verena, and the adopted child, Gautier]. 3. A German colonist from the dismissed Regiment de Meuron. 4. A Scottish Highland Colonist. 5. A colonist wandered in from French Canada." Mrs. Elizabeth Eames, a descendant of Rindisbacher, believes that No. 4, a young man holding a rifle and talking to the Swiss colonist, may be the nineteen-year-old Peter. The fourth Canadian work that may contain a self-view of the artist is his watercolor of Governor Bulger greeting the Red Lake Chippewas outside Fort Douglas; a figure in a top hat and moccasins. (The only representation that Peter is definitely known to have made of himself is his self-portrait, which he painted apparently later in life, probably in St. Louis).

59) The *Neue Zürcher Zeitung* account of Rindisbacher's life (April 14, 1870) says that, from the time of Peter's arrival in Canada, he had planned to produce "a natural history of northern America," but that, "although he made a diligent effort to produce a fine work, his untimely death prevented its completion." He did do many drawings of animals and birds and may have had plans somewhat like those of Audubon.

60) "I at Home," Part VIII, the diary of Stephen Hempstead, Sr., edited by Mrs. Dana O. Jensen, in the Missouri Historical Society *Bulletin*, Vol. 22, No. 2, Part 1 (January, 1966), gives a number of references to the movement of Fever River settlers during the Winnebago "trouble." See entries under July 10, 14, 15, 16, 31 and September 2, 18, 27, 1827.

61) In 1828 President John Quincy Adams had appointed Menard and General McNeil as a two-man commission, but they had disagreed over procedures, and in 1829 Jackson added Atwater to the group. In an article of reminiscences on Colonel Henry Gratiot in the Wisconsin State Historical *Collections*, Vol. X (1883-1885), p. 251, E. B. Washburne, who recalled Atwater's visit to the Galena area after the signing of the Prairie de Chien treaty, described the Circleville lawyer as a "weak and inoffensive old man from Ohio." That impression, however, undoubtedly, resulted from the fact that Atwater became seriously ill after the treaty session and was so indisposed that he scarcely had the strength to travel from day to day.

62) "I at Home," Part IX, the diary of Stephen Hempstead, Sr., ed. by Mrs. Dana O. Jensen, Missouri Historical Society *Bulletin*, Vol. 22, No. 4, Part 1 (July, 1966), p. 417.

63) *Ibid.*, pp. 418-419. This diary account says only that Charles's possessions were put aboard the *Missouri* on June 29. But in Atwater's *Remarks made on a Tour to Prairie Du Chien . . .*, Columbus, Ohio, 1831, the author noted that he and the other members of the Commission left St. Louis on June 30. He does not mention Rindisbacher, although he says that many passengers for Galena and Prairie du Chien were aboard.

64) Atwater, *Writings* (Columbus, 1833), pp. 247-248. The *Tour* was first published in 1831.

65) On June 1, 1831, in Washington, Atwater had noted in a letter, published in the *New York Observer* on August 27, 1831: "I have a beautiful drawing of a [muskrat] taken in that country by an artist residing at Gratiot's Grove." See "Peter Rindisbacher: Frontier Reporter" by John Francis McDermott, *The Art Quarterly*, Detroit Institute of Arts, Vol. XII, No. 2 (Spring, 1949), p. 144, n. 9.

66) "Peter Rindisbacher: A Communication," by Alice E. Smith, *Minnesota History*, Vol. 20 (June, 1939), pp. 173-174. After the signing of the treaty at Prairie du Chien, Atwater traveled overland by wagon with Henry Gratiot on the east side of the Mississippi River to Dodge's mines at Dodgeville, then to Gratiot's Grove, Galena, and Edwardsville, and across country to Vincennes and Louisville. The three small paintings are still owned by the State Historical Society of Wisconsin at Madison. As stated, the fate of the fourth is presently not known.

67) Alice E. Smith, *Minnesota History*, Vol. 20 (June, 1939), p. 174.

68) In a footnote to their work, McKenney and Hall commented that "the person from whom we received the painting of the War Dance stated it to be a representation of a war dance of the Sauks and Foxes. This was an error, which we now correct." McKenney and Hall were wrong; the information from the original informant was correct.

69) McKenney and Hall, *The Indian Tribes of North America*, ed. by Frederick Webb Hodge, Vol. I, Edinburgh, 1933, p. 2.

70) See McDermott, p. 144, n. 10.

71) Alice E. Smith, *Minnesota History*, Vol. 20 (June, 1939), p. 175.

72) See note 70 above.

73) McKenney and Hall, ed. by Hodge, Vol. I, p. 4.

74) See note 70 above.

75) "A Rindisbacher Water Color," by Grace Lee Nute, *Minnesota History*, Vol. 23 (June, 1942), p. 155.

76) McKenney and Hall, ed. by Hodge, Vol. II, pp. 4-5.

77) Biographical notes on Peter's youngest brother, Frederic, in a *History of Jo Daviess County*, published in Galena, 1878, say that Frederic and his parents moved from the Wisconsin lead country to St. Louis in 1829, so perhaps all the Rindisbachers made the move to St. Louis that year. Frederic and his parents, the biography adds, remained in St. Louis until 1838, when they returned to the Galena area. However, Peter's mother, according to other evidence, died about 1836 and was buried at Gratiot's Grove.

78) Chetlain, *Red River Colony*, Chicago, 1893, p. 36.

79) I am grateful for the efforts of George R. Brooks, Director, and Mrs. Frances H. Stadler, Archivist, of the Missouri Historical Society in searching for the identity of this "portrait painter of some note."

80) See note 78 above.

81) McDermott, in *The Art Quarterly*, Spring, 1949, p. 138, cites a letter written from Washington on September 17, 1829, and states that an excerpt from it was printed in the *St. Louis Beacon*, December 12, 1829. The same letter, but dated October 17, 1829, was printed in part in the *Turf Register*, February 1830, p. 308.

82) See also McDermott comments, *The Art Quarterly*, cited in note 65 above, p. 138 and p. 144, n. 11.

83) As pointed out by McDermott, p. 144, n. 11, the writer could not have been Atwater, who had not yet reached Washington from Prairie du Chien — unless the letter was misdated.

84) This and the following information was first summarized and published by McDermott in his 1949 Detroit *Art Quarterly* article, pp. 138-144, and I am indebted to him.

85) Holmes was dead, and in November, 1833, Mason had been transferred from Jefferson Barracks to Fort Gibson in present-day Oklahoma.

86) In April, 1840, *Burton's Gentleman's Magazine* also ran a sketch by Rindisbacher. See Nute, *Minnesota History*, Vol. 14, No. 3 (September, 1933), p. 287, which cites "Villages of the Algonquian, Siouan, and Caddoan Tribes West of the Mississippi" by David I. Bushnell, Jr., Bureau of American Ethnology *Bulletin No. 77*, Washington, D.C., 1922.

87) Personal correspondence to the author from Mrs. Frances H. Stadler, Missouri Historical Society, March 14, 1969.

88) McDermott, p. 142. See also McDermott's reference in the same place to a miniature of Wilson Primm, believed to have been done in 1828.

89) Missouri Historical Society *Bulletin*, October, 1952, referred to in letter to the author from Mrs. Stadler, March 14, 1969. Both the Schirmer and Monnier (spelled Monier in 1821 Berne passport) families had gone from Switzerland to Red River with the Rindisbachers and had then come to the United States. Peter's sister, Christina, married Charles Monnier.

90) Letter from Mrs. Stadler, March 14, 1969.

91) William Clark's estate inventory did not list a Rindisbacher painting, and there is no evidence that he had ever owned a Rindisbacher work. But the inventory of the estate of William Preston Clark, second son of the explorer who died on May 16, 1840, "of apoplexy," includes "4 paintings of Rindisbacher," framed, and valued at $2.00! According to Mrs. Stadler of the Missouri Historical Society, who kindly furnished me with this information, most of the items listed in the W. P. Clark estate inventory "have a penciled notation of price, undoubtedly what they brought at auction, but the Rindisbachers were initialed MLC, which is explained in a note on the inventory to mean that they were 'received by M. L. Clark' (Meriwether Lewis Clark, oldest son of William)." Letter from Mrs. Stadler to the author, May 17, 1969.

92) They are now a part of the Northern Natural Gas Company Collection at the Joslyn Art Museum in Omaha.

93) McDermott, p. 142.

94) Letter from Mrs. Stadler to the author, March 14, 1969.

95) Doctors with whom I have discussed this question tend to think that Peter may have died of a heart attack, since a person with cholera usually went through a protracted period of severe symptoms before dying. It should be noted, at the same time, that, according to Mrs. Eames, a descendant of Peter's brother, Frederic, various other versions of Peter's death exist among present-day members of the Rindisbacher family, although none of them are supported by any known documentary evidence. One story, quite persistent, is that Peter had married — possibly an Indian girl, possibly a halfblood, or, in one version, a French girl from New Orleans. Whoever she was, she did not receive the approval of the rest of the family. One story says that she poisoned the artist and caused his death. Another says that she, the artist, and their twin children all died of cholera in 1834. All that can be said with any certainty, however, is that family folklore about Peter hints strongly that he had a wife and was not on the best of terms with all the other members of his family when he died. If this were true, that fact, too, would have contributed to the veil of obscurity that has hidden information about him.

96) Note the discrepancy in the date of death between this newspaper account and the record in the St. Louis Grays' Minute Book.

97) Peter Sr. died in Jo Daviess County, Illinois, on February 8, 1865, and was buried at Stockton in that county. (About 1937, however, a man who said he was a grandson of Peter Sr. informed Alice E. Smith of the State Historical Society of Wisconsin that the old pioneer and father of the artist had died "about 1870, and was buried under what is now the main street of Shullsburg, Wisconsin." See *Minnesota History*, June, 1939, p. 175). The man who spoke with Alice E. Smith has since been identified as C. H. Rindesbacher of Minoqua, Wisconsin, a great grandson of Peter Sr. The artist's mother, as previously stated, died about 1836 and was buried at Gratiot's Grove. Of Peter's brothers and sisters, Anna Barbara is known to have married Dr. Louis Ostertag, one of the Swiss emigrants to Red River, and, after his death, a Mr. William Collins; Christina married Charles Monnier; and Magdalena married Robert Oliver. A number of Peter's drawings and paintings were passed on to their descendants, as well as to those of Frederic, the brother who had been born at Red River, and who in 1857 — after a stint at the California mines during the gold rush — married Alvira Claypool and settled down as a farmer in Jo Daviess County. Many of Peter's works are still owned by family members, some of whom now spell the name Rindesbacher. But others of the artist's works, which Peter Sr. passed on to the artist's brothers and sisters, are apparently gone forever. In 1969, one descendant revealed to Mrs. Elizabeth Eames that when he was a young man "all the young children used to draw on the backs of the artist's sketches and cut them up with scissors to make paper dolls!" And furthermore, when his grandmother, Frederic's wife, Alvira, died, he himself threw out a large box of sketches and paints — "just old pieces of paper with drawings by Francis and we didn't think they were worth anything!" (Letter from Elizabeth Eames to Mitchell Wilder, Amon Carter Museum, May 5, 1969).

98) See Heilmaier's translation in "Peter Rindisbacher, Swiss Artist," *Minnesota History*, Vol. 32 (September, 1951), p. 156.

BIBLIOGRAPHY

Adams, Mrs. Ann. "Early Days at Red River Settlement, and Fort Snelling..." Minnesota Historical Society *Collections*, Vol. 6 (1894), pp. 75-115.

American Turf Register & Sporting Magazine: Vol. I, No. 2 (Oct., 1829), pp. 73-74; Vol. I, No. 5 (Jan., 1830), pp. 253-254; Vol. I, No. 6 (Feb., 1830), p. 308; Vol. I, No. 11 (July, 1830), pp. 555-557; Vol. III, No. 6 (Feb. 1832), pp. 296-297; Vol. III, No. 12 (August, 1832), pp. 589-591; Vol. IV, No. 2 (Oct., 1832), pp. 57-59; Vol. IV, No. 4 (Dec., 1832), pp. 161-164; Vol. IV, No. 5 (Jan., 1833), p. 239; Vol. IV, No. 10 (June, 1833), pp. 493, 501, 531-534; Vol. IV, No. 12 (Aug., 1833), pp. 605-606; Vol. V, No. 2 (Oct., 1833), pp. 50, 57; Vol. V, No. 4 (Dec., 1833), pp. 165-166; Vol. XI, (Oct., 1840), pp. 495-496.

Atwater, Caleb. *Remarks made on a Tour to Prairie Du'Chien; thence to Washington City in 1829*. Columbus, Ohio, 1831. Reprinted as part of the same author's *The Writings of Caleb Atwater*. Columbus, 1833.

Bryce, George, and Bell, C. N. "Original Letters and Other Documents Relating to the Selkirk Settlement..." The Historical and Scientific Society of Manitoba *Transactions No. 33*, Winnipeg, 1889.

Burton's Gentleman's Magazine, April, 1840.

Bushnell, David I., Jr. "Villages of the Algonquian, Siouan, and Caddoan Tribes West of the Mississippi," Bureau of American Ethnology *Bulletin No. 77*, Washington, D. C., 1922.

Campbell, Marjorie Wilkins. *The North West Company*. St. Martin's Press, New York, 1957, pp. 198-280.

Campbell, Robert. "Account of the early Settlement of the Red River ... by one who was there." Manuscript written in 1892. Courtesy Minnesota Historical Society, St. Paul.

Catlin, George. *Letters and Notes on the Manners, Customs, and Condition of the North American Indians*. Vol. I, New York, 1842.

Chetlain, Augustus L. "The Red River Colony," *Harper's New Monthly Magazine*, Vol. 58 (December, 1878), pp. 47-55.

______. *The Red River Colony*. Chicago, 1893.

Davis, Frank. "Early Days in Canada." *The Illustrated London News*, October 10, 1964, p. 568.

"The Diary of John Corcoran — Voyage from the Red River in Hudson's Bay Territory to St. Louis, Missouri, in the Year 1827," ed. Charles van Ravenswaay, Missouri Historical Society *Bulletin*, April, 1957, pp. 264-274.

Dictionary of American Biography.

Dunbabin, Thomas. "Captain Lyon in the Arctic," *The Beaver*, Spring, 1963, pp. 45-51.

Ewers, John C. "Charles Bird King, Painter of Indian Visitors to the Nation's Capital," *Smithsonian Institution Report for 1953*, Washington, D. C., 1854, pp. 463-473.

______. "George Catlin, Painter of Indians and the West," *Smithsonian Institution Report for 1955*, Washington, 1956, pp. 483-528.

______. *Artists of the Old West*. Doubleday and Company, Inc., Garden City, N. Y., 1965, pp. 53-64.

Finlayson, Isobel. "York Boat Journal," Intro. Alice M. Johnson. *The Beaver*, Sept., 1951, pp. 32-35; Dec. 1951, pp. 32-37.

Folwell, William W. *A History of Minnesota*. Vol. I, St. Paul, 1921.

Gressley, Gene M. "The Red River settlement: chaos and emerging order," *North Dakota History*, Vol. 27, Oct., 1960, pp. 153-166.

Hansen, Marcus L. *Old Fort Snelling, 1819-1858*. (reprint ed.), Minneapolis, 1958.

Hedlin, Ralph. "Port of the Pioneers," *The Beaver*, Winter, 1957, pp. 44-49.

Hempstead, Stephen, Sr. "I at Home," ed. Mrs. Dana O. Jensen, Missouri Historical Society *Bulletin*, Vol. 22, No. 2, Part 1, Jan., 1966, pp. 180-206; Vol. 22, No. 4, Part 1, July, 1966, pp. 410-445.

Heron, Francis. "The Record Flood of 1826," intro. Clifford Wilson, *The Beaver*, Sept., 1950, pp. 42-46.

History of Joe Daviess County. Galena, Ill., 1878.

Howard, Joseph Kinsey. *Strange Empire*. William Morrow, New York, 1952, pp. 32-45.

Jackson, Donald (ed.). *Black Hawk, an Autobiography*. Urbana, Ill., 1955.

Jones, Evan. *Citadel in the Wilderness.* Coward-McCann, New York, 1966.

Kurz, Rudolph F. "Journal of Rudolph Freiderich Kurz . . . 1846-1852," trans. Myrtis Jarrell; ed. J. N. P. Hewitt, Bureau of American Ethnology *Bulletin 115*, Washington, D. C., 1937.

Leechman, Douglas. "The Trappers," *The Beaver*, Winter, 1957, pp. 24-31.

McCracken, Harold. *Portrait of the Old West.* McGraw-Hill, New York, 1952, pp. 43-44.

McDermott, John Francis. "Peter Rindisbacher: Frontier Reporter," *The Art Quarterly*, Detroit Institute of Arts, Vol. 12, No. 2, Spring, 1949, pp. 129-145.

McKenney, Thomas L., and Hall, James. *History of the Indian Tribes of North America, with Biographical Sketches and Anecdotes of the Principal Chiefs*, 3 vols., Philadelphia, 1837. Republished, with added notes, ed. Frederick Webb Hodge and David I. Bushnell, Jr., Edinburgh, Scotland, 1933.

MacLeod, Margaret Arnett. "The Company in Winnipeg," *The Beaver*, Sept., 1940, pp. 6-11.

______. Nute, Grace Lee; and Wilson, Clifford. "Peter Rindisbacher, Red River Artist," *The Beaver*, Dec., 1945, pp. 30-36.

______. "Winnipeg and the HBC," *The Beaver*, June, 1949, pp. 3-7.

May, Rudolf von. *Kurze und Wahre Uebersicht aller de Vortheile, welche ein Ansiedler in der Kolonie des Rothen-Flusses in Nordamerika glegen, zu erwarter und zu geniessen hat*, Berne, Switzerland, 1820.

Merk, Frederick. *Fur Trade and Empire.* Cambridge, Mass., 1931.

Meuli, Karl. "Peter Rindisbacher, The Indian Painter from Emmenthal," *Reiträge zur Volkskunde*, Basel, Switzerland, 1960, pp. 140-174.

Milwaukee Journal, December 3, 1967.

Missouri Republican, St. Louis, August 15, 1834.

"Mrs. Adéle P. Gratiot's Narrative," Wisconsin State Historical *Collections*, Vol. 10, 1883-1885, pp. 261-275.

Murray, Charles Augustus. *Travels in North America During the Years 1834, 1835, & 1836.* Vol. II. London, R. Bentley, 1839.

Neue Zürcher Zeitung, Zurich, Switzerland, Nos. 187 and 189, April 13, 14, 1870: "Rindisbacher, The Painter" by "F. M." Trans. Anna M. Heilmaier, intro. Michel Benisovich ("Peter Rindisbacher, Swiss Artist"), *Minnesota History*, Vol. 32, Sept., 1951, pp. 155-162.

"News and Comment," *Minnesota History*, Vol. 23, March, 1942, p. 94.

New York Observer, August 27, 1831.

Nichols, Roger L. "General Henry Atkinson and the Building of Jefferson Barracks," Missouri Historical Society *Bulletin*, Vol. 22, No. 3, April, 1966, pp. 321-326.

Nute, Grace Lee. "Peter Rindisbacher, Artist," *Minnesota History*, Vol. 14, No. 3, Sept., 1933, pp. 283-287.

______. "Rindisbacher's Minnesota Water Colors," *Minnesota History*, Vol. 20, March, 1939, pp. 54-57.

______. "A Rindisbacher Water Color," *Minnesota History*, Vol. 23, 1942, pp. 154-156.

Pestalozzi, F. O. "Peter Rindisbacher" in Brun, Carl, *Schweizer Kuenstler-Lexikon*, Vol. 2, 1908, p. 630.

Pritchett, John P. *The Red River Valley, 1811-1849: a regional study.* New Haven, Conn., 1942.

Rich, E. E. *The History of the Hudson's Bay Company, 1670-1870*, Vol. II, London, 1959.

"Rindisbacher," Notes, *The Beaver*, Sept., 1946, p. 50.

Robinson, Doane. *A History of the Dakota or Sioux Indians*, (reprint ed.), Minneapolis, 1956.

Ross, Alexander. *The Red River Settlement: its rise, progress and present state.* London, 1856.

______. "Settlers at Red River" (excerpts from his book), *The Beaver*, Sept., 1952, pp. 32-35.

Scanlan, Peter L. *Prairie du Chien, French, British, American.* Menasha, Wisc., 1937.

Shave, Harry. "Centenary of a Diocese," *The Beaver*, Sept., 1949, pp. 4-7.

______. "John West, Peguis and P. Rindisbacher," *The Beaver*, Summer, 1957, pp. 14-19.

Smith, Alice E. "Peter Rindisbacher; A Communication," *Minnesota History*, Vol. 20, June, 1939, pp. 173-175.

"Some New Rindisbachers," unsigned, *The Beaver*, June, 1950, pp. 14-15.

Stanley, George F. G. "A Soldier at Fort Garry," *The Beaver*, Autumn, 1957, pp. 10-15.

St. Louis Beacon, December 12, 1829.

St. Louis Times, April 30, 1831.

Lawrence Taliaferro Papers. Microfilm copies of originals at Minnesota Historical Society, St. Paul.

Tribolet, H. "Peter Rindisbacher" in *Dictionnaire historique et biographique de la Suisse*. Vol. 5, Neuchâtel, 1929, p. 636.

Tuckerman, Henry T. *Book of the Artists*. New York, 1867, p. 632.

Warner, Oliver. "Voyaging to York Factory," *The Beaver*, Winter, 1957, pp. 22-23.

Washburne, E. B. "Col. Henry Gratiot," Wisconsin State Historical *Collections*, Vol. 10, 1883-1885, pp. 233-260.

West, John. *The Substance of a Journal during a Residence at the Red River Colony, British North America*. L. B. Seeley and Son, London, 1824.

Wilson, Clifford. "Peter Rindisbacher, First Western Artist," *Canadian Art*, No. 83, Jan.-Feb., 1963, pp. 50-53.

INDEX

OTHER PUBLICATIONS OF THE AMON CARTER MUSEUM INCLUDE:

PAPER TALK
Illustrated Letters of Charles M. Russell
Introduction and Commentary by Frederic G. Renner

THE ARTIST'S ENVIRONMENT: WEST COAST
Text by Frederick S. Wight

APPALOOSA
The Spotted Horse in Art and History
Text by Francis Haines

TAOS AND SANTA FE
The Artist's Environment, 1882-1942
Text by Van Deren Coke

FRONTIER GUNS
Commentary by John Graves

WALT KUHN
An Imaginary History of the West
Foreword by Fred S. Bartlett

SANTOS
The Religious Folk Art of New Mexico
Essay by George Kubler

PETER HURD
A Portrait Sketch from Life
Text by Paul Horgan

STANDING UP COUNTRY
The Canyon Lands of Utah & Arizona
Text by Gregory Crampton

TODD WEBB PHOTOGRAPHS
Early Western Trails and Some Ghost Towns
Introduction by Beaumont Newhall

QUIET TRIUMPH
Forty Years with the Indian Arts Fund, Santa Fe

BRETT WESTON PHOTOGRAPHS
Introduction by Nancy Newhall

GEORGIA O'KEEFFE
The Work of the Artist from 1915 to 1966
Commentaries by her Contemporaries

CAMPOSANTOS
A Photographic Essay by Dorothy Benrimo
Commentary by Rebecca Salsbury James
Historical Notes by E. Boyd

T. H. O'SULLIVAN, PHOTOGRAPHER
Text by Beaumont and Nancy Newhall
Published in Collaboration with George Eastman House

TEXAS HOMES OF THE 19TH CENTURY
Photographs by Todd Webb
Text by Drury Blakeley Alexander

CHARLES M. RUSSELL
Paintings, Drawings and Sculpture in the Amon G. Carter Collection
A Descriptive Catalogue by Frederic G. Renner

AUNT CLARA
The Paintings of Clara McDonald Williamson
Text by Donald and Margaret Vogel

PAINTING IN TEXAS: THE NINETEENTH CENTURY
Text by Pauline A. Pinckney
Introduction by Jerry Bywaters

DOROTHEA LANGE LOOKS AT THE AMERICAN COUNTRY WOMAN
A Photographic Essay by Dorothea Lange
Commentary by Beaumont Newhall

BARTLETT'S WEST
Drawing the Mexican Boundary
Text by Robert V. Hine

CUSTER'S LAST
or The Battle of the Little Big Horn
Text by Don Russell

THE TRACK GOING BACK
A Century of Transcontinental Railroading, 1869-1969
Text by Everett L. DeGolyer, Jr.

THE WILD WEST
A History of the Wild West Shows
Text by Don Russell

Lithography: The Meriden Gravure Company, Meriden, Connecticut   Design: Crawford Dunn Associates, Dallas, Texas